THE BEST 500 PUB JOKES

THIS IS A CARLTON BOOK

Text and design copyright © 1999, 2009 Carlton Books Ltd

This edition published by Carlton Books Limited 2009

ISBN 978-1-85375-735-8

Printed in the UK by CPI Mackays, Chatham, ME5 8TD

The text in this book first appeared in *The Best Pub Joke Book Ever! 2*

THE BEST 500 PUB JOKES

TIM DEDOPULOS

PRION

Contents

Introduction

Everybody likes a laugh. I certainly do; there are no lengths I wouldn't go to in order to track down a funny joke. In the course of assembling the jokes to go into this book, I've been forced to do all sorts of things that would normally be against my moral and religious principles. There were long, dangerous treks into the uncharted wilderness, for example. Arduous journeys that took me deep into territory known only to savage primitive warriors, where I cunningly drew upon my training to infiltrate ancient temples, eavesdropping on unhallowed rituals. I wouldn't be exagerrating if I said that my life would have been forfeit had I been discovered.

Still, I made it back out again, with a prize stash of jokes under my arm, and all it cost me was a taxi fare and a few rounds. You might think I'm over-estimating the danger, but Popley is a scary place if you're an outsider. The Basingstoke planning council needed to divide it into districts, but rather than call it Upper Popley, Long Popley, Popley Downs and so on, as everyone else does, they just numbered it - Popley 1 through to Popley 6. To get in and out of Popley 3 without being filled in takes luck, skill and dedication.

Then there were the months I spent with the nomads of the plain, learning their ways and tales and undergoing initiatory rites. A wizened shaman took me into his care, imparting generations of tribal gags, so that they would be preserved the next time the police bust them up and moved them on. He escorted me to a mighty gathering, but it was really muddy again, so he buggered off on the Sunday morning muttering about a little stretch of wood outside Devizes.

There are other tales I could tell. Once or twice I even had to abandon all my principles completely and do some work, horrific as it may sound. Anyway, the point is that in this book are more than 1000 jokes collected over literally whole weeks down the pub drinking. Reading and knowing them won't make you a better person, necessarily, but they will make you a funnier one. If you ration yourself to cracking just two a night, you've got more than a year's worth of material - enough to grant you legendary status. After all, how many people do you know who can come up with two new jokes every night for a year? Play your cards right and people will be buying you drinks as you walk through the door, so that they can be the first to share your new gems of humour. Members of the opposite sex will be desperate to seduce you to learn your secrets. You'll be first in line for the job of President For Life if we ever become a dictatorship.

Perhaps.

Still, even if you only get a laugh, and not a pint, a shag or a country, it's still a result.

Animal Magic

1

Jokes about the
Natural World

A vicar wanted to buy a parrot. "Are you sure it doesn't swear?" he asked the storekeeper. "Oh, absolutely. It's a religious parrot," the storekeeper assured him. "Do you see those strings on his legs? When you pull the right one he recites the Lord's Prayer, and when you pull on the left one he chants the 23rd Psalm." "That's wonderful!" said the vicar, reaching for his chequebook, "and what happens if you pull both strings?" "I fall off my fucking perch, you piece of shit!" screeched the parrot.

Two soldiers stationed in the Falklands were handed spades and told to bury a large, dead animal. While they were digging, they got into an argument about exactly what it was they were burying. "This is a bloody big mule!" "It isn't a mule, you idiot, it's a donkey." "Mule!" "Donkey!" "Mule!" "Donkey!" They went on like this for a while until the camp chef came out to see what the noise was. "What are you lads up to?" he asked. "We're diggin' a grave for this mule," said the first. "Donkey, dammit!" replied the other. The chef cut in, "Lads, this isn't either. It's an ass." An hour later, the commander of the garrison came up and said, "What are you men digging, a foxhole?" They nodded respectfully, then the first one said "No, sir! We're digging an asshole, sir!"

****

Why do birds fly south? Because it's just too far to walk.

****

A farmer, upset at the small number of eggs that his hens were laying, decided to go to town to buy a fresh cockerel who could liven things up a bit. Down at the supply shop, the bloke behind the counter apologised; all he had was one incredible randy cockerel. "But that's just what I need!" the farmer said. "Not this cockerel," said the bloke, "he's trouble. I've never seen anything so sex-obsessed." But the farmer insisted, and eventually agreed to buy the cockerel on the condition that he wouldn't ever bring him back into the town, let alone return him to the shop. Once back at the farm, the cockerel immediately jumped into the hen-house and shagged every hen repeatedly until they were all exhausted and near death. Undaunted, the cockerel then hopped the fence, got in with the ducks and fucked all of them unconscious. He then leaped another fence and proceeded to decimate the geese. This continued for three days until the farm had been devastated. That afternoon the farmer found the cockerel flat out in the middle of the yard, with buzzards circling overhead. "Serves you right, you filthy little bastard," said the farmer, at which point the cockerel pointed up at the sky, winked and said, "Shhhhhhhhh."

****

Why do hens lay eggs? It's obvious. If they dropped them, they'd break.

****

A pair of chickens walk up to the withdrawals desk at a public library and say, 'Buk Buk BUK.' Deciding that the chickens want three books, the librarian hands some over and the chickens cluck in thanks and leave. Around midday, the chickens come back to the desk and say, 'Buk Buk BuKKOOK!' The librarian passes over another three books and the chickens leave as before. The chickens then return to the library in the early afternoon, approach the librarian and, looking very annoyed, cluck, 'Buk Buk Buk Buk Bukkooook!' The librarian is by now a bit suspicious of these chickens, so she gives them a further five books, and decides to follow them. Trailing at a safe distance, she follows them out of the library, out through the town centre and to a park. Hiding behind a tree, she peeks out at the birds, who head down to the pond. When they get to the water's edge, she's horrified to see them throw all the books into the water. Suddenly, they come flying back out again and this frog sticks its head up and, in a smug tone of voice, says "Rrredit Rrredit Rrredit Rrredit Rrredit..."

****

Is it polite to eat fried chicken with your fingers? No. You should always eat your fingers separately.

****

What do you get when you cross a chick with an alley cat? A peeping tom.

****

This bloke with a parrot is getting married. On the day of the wedding, he says, "Listen, I know you're always in that bloody window. My wife and I are coming back here to pack after the wedding, and no matter what you hear, do not turn around or I'll break your damned neck! We want some privacy!" The parrot reluctantly agrees. The happy couple then come back from the wedding and start packing, but they can't get the suitcase closed. "Get on top," says the bloke, "that'll do it." She gives it a shot, but despite much effort and grunting it doesn't close. His wife then says, "Look, you get on top, that'll be better." They heave away again, with no luck. Finally, the bloke says, "I tell you what, let's both get on top; that should fix it!" The parrot immediately turns around and says, "Neck or no neck, I have got to see this!"

****

Diner: Do you serve chicken here? Waiter: Sit down, sir. We serve anyone.

****

What do you get when you cross a parrot with a centipede? A walkie-talkie.

****

An elderly lady buys a pair of parrots, but she cannot identify their sexes. She calls the pet shop, and the man there advises her to watch them carefully and all will become clear in time. She spends weeks staring at the cage, and eventually catches them shagging. To make sure she doesn't get them mixed up again, she cuts a ring out from a piece of cardboard and puts it round the male parrot's neck. The following week, the local vicar calls in for a cup of tea. He's just making himself comfortable when the male parrot notices his dog-collar. "Eh up," leered the parrot, "Who did she catch you screwing?"

****

Kath was expecting the plumber. He was supposed to arrive at ten o'clock. Ten o'clock came and went - no plumber. Eleven o'clock, twelve o'clock, and one o'clock sailed past, still with no plumber. She decided he wasn't coming, and went out to do some chores. Naturally, no sooner had she left than the plumber arrived. He knocked on the door and, from the lounge, Kath's parrot called, "Who is it?" Presuming the parrot to be the lady of the house he called back, "It's the plumber," and waited for her to come and let him in. When no-one opened the door, he knocked again. Again the parrot called, "Who is it?" Frustrated, he yelled, "It's the plumber!" He waited some more, and again no-one came to the door. He knocked again, long and hard. Again the parrot called, "Who is it?" and he shouted, "IT'S THE PLUMBER!" Once again he waited, and again she didn't come. Furious at the way she was taking the piss, he hammered on the door again and again. The parrot, who was having a great time, called, "Who is it?" innocently. It was too much for the plumber, who went berserk. With a loud scream he took a wrench to the lock, hammered it to bits and broke the door down. The excitement proved too much for the poor bloke, though, and he had a massive heart attack, dropping dead in the hall. When Kath got back an hour later she found the door ripped open and a corpse lying in the doorway. "Fuck!" she shrieked, "WHO IS IT?" Gleefully, the parrot howled "IT'S THE PLUMBER!"

Diner: I can't eat this chicken. Call the manager. Waiter: It's no use, sir. He can't eat it either.

Which side of a chicken has the most feathers? The outside.

****

When her dishwasher packed up, Mrs Williams phoned the repair man. He couldn't accommodate her request for an after-hours appointment, and because she had to go to work she told him, "I'll leave the key under the mat. Fix the dishwasher, leave your invoice on the counter and I'll post you a cheque. By the way, I have a large Rottweiler called Fang, but don't worry, he's very well-trained and he won't bother you. I also have a large parrot. Whatever you do, no matter what he says to you, do not say anything to the bird!" Well, sure enough, the dog totally ignored the repair man, but the whole time he was there the parrot swore, yelled, screamed and just about drove the bloke mad. As he was getting ready to leave, he just couldn't resist saying to the parrot, "You stupid fucking mangy ball of feathers, shut the fuck up!" The bird went quiet for a moment, fixed him with a malicious glare, then shouted at the top of its voice: "Kill, Fang. Kill, boy!"

****

Two morons are standing on a cliff with their arms outstretched. One has some budgies lined up on his arms, and the other has parrots tied to his. After a couple of minutes they leap off the cliff and splat! Lying next to each other in intensive care at the hospital, the first moron says to the second one, "I don't think much of this budgie jumping." The other moron replies, "Yeah, I'm not too keen on this parrotgliding either."

****

Two tall trees are growing in the woods. A small tree begins to grow up between them. One turns to the other and says, "Is that a son of a beech, or a son of a birch?" The other says he cannot tell. When a woodpecker lands on the small tree, the first big tree says, "Woodpecker, you're a tree expert. Can you tell if that is a son of a beech or a son of a birch?" The woodpecker takes a taste of the small tree, and replies, "It is neither a son of a beech nor a son of a birch. That, gentlemen, is the best piece of ash I have ever had my pecker in!"

****

A farmer was sitting in his farmyard eating a sandwich when a hen zoomed by, with a cockerel in hot pursuit and closing fast. Suddenly the cockerel slammed on the anchors, screeched to a halt and began pecking at the crumbs from the sandwich. "Damn," muttered the farmer, "I hope I never get that hungry!"

****

A bloke walks into a pet shop and asks if he can buy a canary. The proprietor replies, "I'm sorry, we've sold out. You won't find a canary in town. I do have a parakeet, though." The bloke insists he wants a canary, so the shop owner tells him that a parakeet can be made to sound just like a canary if you file the beak down. "But you have to be careful not to file too much off, or the parakeet will drown when he goes to take a drink of water." The bloke reckons that this is complete bullshit, but thanks the shop owner politely and leaves. He goes into another pet shop and asks for a canary, but again he has no luck. "But", says the girl behind the counter, "I do have a parakeet, and if you file the beak down carefully it can be made to sound just like a canary." She, too, then goes on to explain that filing off too much beak will jeopardise the bird's life, due to the potential for drowning. The bloke decides that there might be something to it, and buys the parakeet. "Besides", he tells himself, "parakeets are much cheaper." His next stop is a hardware shop, where he wanders into the tools section, holding his recently-purchased bird. The owner wanders by and asks if he needs some help. The bloke sheepishly explains how he intends to make his parakeet sing like a canary. The hardware store owner knowingly picks up a file and hands it to him. "Here, this is what you want - a Simonson No.5 rough-edged file. But be careful not to file too much off, or the poor thing will drown." The bloke thanks the hardware store owner, pays up and leaves for home. A few weeks later, the bloke wanders into the hardware store again. The owner, recognising him, asks how it went with the parakeet. The bloke looks down and sadly reports, "Actually, the bird's dead." The hardware store owner looks sympathetic and asks, "Did you file off too much beak?" The bloke shakes his head and says, "Nope. He was dead when I took him out of the vice."

****

Have you heard about that disease that you get from shagging birds? Chirpes? It's one of those canarial diseases. I hear it's untweetable.

****

Some feline definitions - Human being: An automatic door opener for cats. Purranoia: The fear that your cat is up to something. Purring: The sound of a cat making cuteness. Purrpetual motion: A kitten at play. Purrverse: Poem about a kinky cat. Pussy Whip: The dessert topping for cats.

****

How do you make a cat go woof? Douse it in petrol and throw a match at it. How do you make a dog go meow? Freeze it solid in the freezer, then take a chainsaw to it.

****

Radioactive cats have 18 half-lives.

****

Cats know how we feel. They don't give a damn, but they know.

****

Cats took many thousands of years to domesticate humans.

****

Dogs come when called. Cats take a message and get back to you.

****

It's really the cat's house. I just pay the mortgage.

****

Do not meddle in the affairs of cats, for they are subtle and will piss on your computer.

****

According to an animal protection group in Jerusalem, there have been many recent cases of people throwing cats out of cars, apparently in an attempt to abandon them to the streets...

****

A bloke is in his back garden one lazy Sunday afternoon when he hears some crunching next door. Being nosy, he looks over the fence and sees his neighbour digging a hole in his garden. Naturally, he asks what the hole is for. "My canary died and I'm burying it," said the neighbour. "Oh, I'm sorry about that," says the bloke insincerely. "That's a pretty big hole for a canary, isn't it?" he added. "Well, yes," replies the neighbour, "but it's inside your fucking cat!"

****

Janet went to a bridge club every Thursday night, and after a peaceful game or two with the ladies she would return home to fix her husband dinner when he got home from the pub. One Thursday she was playing a great game, and had an incredible hand, when she noticed the time. "Oh, no! I have to go fix my husband his dinner! He's going to be so angry if it's not ready on time." She dashed out of her friend's house, her great hand forgotten on the table. When she got home, she realised she had very little food in the cupboard and not enough time to go to the grocery store. All she had was a wilted lettuce leaf, an egg and a can of cat food. In a panic, she opened the can of cat food, stirred in the egg and garnished it with the lettuce leaf just as her husband was pulling up. While she watched in horror he sat down to his dinner - and then she realised he was really enjoying it! "Mmmm, darling, this is the best dinner you've made for me in 40 years of marriage. You can cook this for me whenever you want!" That night they had sex for the first time in months, and it was incredible!

Needless to say, every Thursday from then on she made the cat food dinner for her husband. She told her bridge friends about it and they were horrified. "You're going to kill him," one said. "He's just winding you up," accused another. Janet continued to make him his cat food dinner on a Thursday, and then afterwards they would shag like fiends. Two months later, Janet's husband died. On the Thursday after the funeral, the bridge ladies attacked her for being so callous. "You killed him!" one said. "We told you that feeding him that cat food every week would do him in! How can you just sit there so calmly and play bridge knowing you murdered your husband?" Janet calmly replied, "Ahh, come off it. I didn't kill him. He smashed his skull falling off the mantelpiece while licking his arse."

****

What do you call a cow that has had an abortion? Decalfinated.

****

A New York family bought a ranch out in the West, where they intended to raise cattle. When some stockbroker friends came out for a visit, they asked if the ranch had a name. "Well," said the new cattleman, "I wanted to name it the Bar-J, my wife favoured Suzy-Q, one son liked the Flying-W and the other wanted the Lazy-Y. We argued about it for a bit and then we decided to compromise, so we're calling it the Bar-J-Suzy-Q-Flying-W-Lazy-Y." "But where are all your cattle?" a friend asked. The rancher sighed. "Actually, none survived being branded."

****

Two cows were chatting to each other over the fence between their fields. The first cow said, "I'm telling you, this mad cow disease really scares me. They say it's spreading fast - I heard it hit some cows down on old Patterson's farm." The other cow replied, "Oh, I'm not worried. It doesn't affect us ducks."

****

A tourist went into a restaurant in Spain and ordered the speciality of the house. When his dinner arrived, he asked the waiter what it was. "These, señor," replied the waiter in broken English, "are the cojones - how you say, the testicles - of the bull that was killed in the ring today." The tourist swallowed hard but tasted the dish and, lo and behold, it was delicious. So he went back the next evening and ordered the same item. When it arrived, he had a look and said to the waiter, "These cojones, or whatever you call them...they're much smaller than the ones I had last night." "Si, señor," replied the waiter, "You see, the bull...he does not always lose."

****

A dog is a dog, except when he is facing you. Then, he is Mr. Dog.

****

The more people I meet, the more I like my dog.

****

Old Farmer Giles got a hefty loan from the bank to buy an expensive bull. A few days later the banker dropped by and asked, "So, how's the new bull doing?" Giles looked downcast and said, "The bull ain't doing none too good, see. I got him out there in the pasture with a lovely bunch of young heifers and he don't want nothing to do with 'em." The banker frowned and said, "You'd better call the vet, and I'll come back in a few days." A week later the banker came back and asked, "Well, Giles, how's that bull doing now?" Smiling, Giles said, "A whole bushel better, he be. He's had his way with all of my cows, jumped over the fence, and he's working his way through Silas's cows next door." The banker was much relieved and said, "Great! What did the vet give him?" Giles said, "He gave him some pills." The banker said, "What kind of pills were those?" Giles said, "I don't rightly know, but they had a strange lemony taste."

Outside of a dog, books are a man's best friend. Inside of a dog, it's too dark and cramped to read.

What is the difference between a poodle humping your leg and a pit-bull humping your leg? The pit-bull gets to finish...

What is meaner than a pit-bull with AIDS? Whatever gave it AIDS in the first place.

Did you hear about the new breed of dog? They crossed a pit bull with a collie, and came up with a long-haired mutt that bites your leg off and then goes for help.

What is the difference between a Rottweiler and a social worker? You can get your children back from a Rottweiler.

What do you do with a dog with no legs? You take it out for a drag.

****

A man went to visit a friend and was amazed to find him playing chess with his dog. He watched the game in astonishment for a while. "I can hardly believe my eyes!" he exclaimed. "That's the smartest dog I've ever seen." His friend shook his head, "Nah, he's not that bright. I beat him three games in five."

****

A blind man with a guide dog walks into a big department store. The man goes to the middle of the department, picks up the dog by the tail and starts swinging it around over his head in circles. The manager, who couldn't fail to see this, is rather upset by the apparent cruelty, so he decides to find out what's going on. He goes up to the blind man and says, "Good afternoon. May I help you?" The blind man shakes his head and says, "No thanks. I'm just looking around."

****

A father gave his teenage daughter a pedigree puppy for her birthday. An hour later when he went to make himself a drink he found her looking at a puddle in the centre of the kitchen. "My pup," she murmured sadly, "runneth over."

****

It was a boring Sunday afternoon in the jungle, so the Elephants decided to challenge the Ants to a game of soccer. The game was going well for the big pachyderms - the Elephants were leading the Ants ten goals to nil - when the Ants gained possession. The Ants' star player was dribbling the ball towards the Elephants' goal when the Elephants' left back came lumbering towards him. The elephant trod on the little ant, killing him instantly. The referee, a monkey, stopped the game. "What the hell do you think you're doing? Do you call that sportsmanship, killing another player?" The elephant replied, "Well, I didn't mean to kill him. I was only trying to trip him up..."

****

Dad, Mum and little Jimmy decide to go to the zoo one day. Eventually they end up at the elephant house. Jimmy looks at the elephant, sees its penis, points to it and says, "Mum, what is that long thing?" His mother replies, "That's the elephant's trunk, Jimmy." "No, at the other end." "That's the elephant's tail." "No, mummy," said Jimmy, "the thing under the elephant." A short embarrassed silence followed, after which she said, "Oh, that's nothing." Mum then went to buy some ice-cream and Jimmy, not being satisfied with her answer, asks Dad the same question. "Dad, what is that long thing?" "That's the elephant's trunk, Jimmy," replied his father. "No, at the other end." "Oh, that's the elephant's tail." "No, dad, the thing below," asked Jimmy in frustration. "Ah. That's the elephant's penis, Jimmy. Why do you ask?" "Well, mum said it was nothing," said Jimmy. Dad shook his head wryly and said, "I tell you, I spoil that woman..."

****

Hickory Dickory Dock, an elephant ran up the clock. The clock is now being repaired.

****

Why are elephants wrinkled? Well, have you ever tried to iron one?

****

What is grey and white on the inside and red on the outside? An elephant turned inside out.

****

An elephant was down by a watering hole having a drink when he saw a turtle out of the corner of his eye. Reacting with immediate swiftness he ran down to the water's edge, jumped up into the air and landed on the turtle, turning it into a revolting pulp. A giraffe standing nearby noticed this and, faintly sickened, asked the elephant why he'd squished the turtle. The elephant calmly replied by saying that particular turtle had bitten him nastily on the trunk some 50 years earlier, with no provocation, and he had now got his revenge. "Wow," said the giraffe, "you must have an incredible memory." The elephant nodded proudly, "Yes, it's turtle recall!"

****

What's the biggest drawback of the jungle? An elephant's foreskin.

****

A guide at the zoo: "Now, ladies and gentlemen, this is the elephant, the largest living animal to roam the earth today. Every day, the elephant eats three dozen bunches of bananas, six tons of hay, and 2,000 pounds of assorted fruits. Madam, please don't stand there...Excuse me, madam, please don't stand near the elephant's backside...Madam, yes, you in the...Madam...Oh, fuck, too late. George, get digging."

****

Have you heard about Hannibal crossing the Alps with elephants? None of the offspring survived.

The United Nations held a competition to discover which nation could produce the best book on elephants. The British submitted a dry historical account, "The Elephant and the British Empire." The French entered a text "The Sensuality of the Elephant - A Personal Account." The Germans submitted an extensive 47-volume work entitled, "An Elementary Introduction to the Foundation of the Science of the Elephant's Trunk." The Americans submitted an article from Money magazine entitled, "Elephants - the Perfect Tax Shelter for the '80s." Sweden commissioned Greenpeace to write a counter-entry "Elephants: They're Better Than People." The Russians put in a terse, melancholy manuscript entitled "The Superiority of the Soviet Elephant," and the Polish submitted a poem, "The Joy and Freedom Brought Forth by the Soviet Elephant." The Greeks sent in a short recipe for clay-baked elephant in a garlic yoghurt sauce, scribbled on the back of a beer-mat. The prize, however, went to the Japanese, for their promotional flyer: "We Have No Elephants, but Wouldn't You Just Love to Buy a Honda Instead?"

****

This tiger woke up one morning and felt just great. He felt so powerful that he went out, cornered a small monkey and roared at him, "Who is the mightiest of all the jungle animals?" The poor quaking little monkey replied, "You are, of course; no one is mightier than you." A little while later, the tiger confronted a deer and bellowed out, "Who is the greatest and strongest of all the jungle animals?" The deer was shaking so hard it could barely speak, but it managed to stammer, "Oh great tiger, you are by far the mightiest animal in the jungle." The tiger, on a roll, then swaggered up to an elephant that was quietly munching on some weeds and roared at the top of his voice, "Who is the mightiest of all the animals in the jungle?" At this, the elephant grabbed the tiger with his trunk, picked him up, slammed him down, picked him up again, shook him until he was just a blur of orange and black and finally threw him violently against a nearby tree. The tiger staggered to his feet, looked up at the elephant and says, "Hey, guy, there's no need to get so wound up just because you don't know the answer."

****

Why was the bluefish blue? Because the blowfish wouldn't.

****

A door-to-door salesman had suffered a really rough day and decided to try one more house before heading home. He knocked on the door, determined that this time he was going to make a sale. He could almost taste it. A boy opened the door and the salesman starts in with his sales pitch. The boy just stood there, speechless, staring at him and the salesman, seeing that he wasn't getting anywhere, asked the boy where his mother was. The boy didn't say a word, he just pointed upstairs. The salesman went up the stairs, opened the bedroom door, and found the boy's mother in bed, fucking a goat! Completely flabbergasted, the salesman slammed the door shut and charged down the stairs. He grabbed the little boy by the shoulders and yelled, "Don't you know what's in bed with your mother? Don't you know what they're doing? Doesn't it bother you?" The boy looked at him, then shook his head and answered, "Na-a-a-a-a-a."

****

What do you get when you cross an onion with a donkey? A piece of ass that'll bring tears to your eyes.

****

Some racehorses are chatting together in a stable. One of them starts to boast about his track record. "Out of my last 15 races, I've won eight!" he says, proudly. Another horse breaks in, "That's good. In my last 27 races, I've won 19!" "Not bad, but out of my last 36 races, I've won 28!" says another, flicking his tail. At this point, they notice a greyhound that has been sitting there listening. "I don't mean to butt in," says the greyhound, "but I've won 88 of my last 90 races." The horses are clearly amazed. "Fuck me!" says one, after a hushed silence. "A talking dog!"

Two cockroaches were munching on garbage in an alley. "I was in that new restaurant across the street," said one. "It's so clean! The kitchen is spotless, the floors are gleaming white. It's so sanitary the whole place shines." "Please," said the other cockroach, frowning, "not while I'm eating!"

****

How do you spot a gay termite? He'll only eat woodpeckers.

****

This termite walks into a pub and says "Is the bar tender here?"

****

Two goldfish in a tank. One turns to the other and says, "So, do you know how to drive this thing?"

****

A chicken and an egg were lying in a post-coital glow. The egg turned to the chicken and said, "Well I think we just answered that old question..."

Two cockney owls were in a bar playing pool, one missed a shot and said to his mate, "That's two 'its mate." His mate replied, "Two 'its to who?"

****

A centipede is an inchworm gone metric.

****

On the most recent flight of the space shuttle, astronauts conducted an important scientific experiment with fruit flies and gleaned a valuable insight. Zero gravity makes the little buggers far easier to swat.

****

A city bloke went out to spend a holiday on a small farm, out in the country. While he was there, he saw the farmer feeding his pigs in a most extraordinary manner. The farmer would lift a pig up to a nearby apple tree and let the pig eat the apples off the tree directly. He moved the pig from one apple to another until the pig was satisfied, then he would start again with another pig. The city man watched this activity for some time with great astonishment. Finally, he could not resist sharing his time management expertise with the farmer, and said, "Forgive me, but that is the most inefficient method of feeding pigs that I can imagine. Just think of the time that would be saved if you simply shook the apples off the tree and let the pigs eat them from the ground!" The farmer looked puzzled, and replied, "What's time to a pig?"

****

How do monkeys pick up rumours? Through the apevine.

****

There was a terrible bus accident. Unfortunately, no one survived except a monkey who was on board, and there were no witnesses. The police tried to investigate further, but got no results. At last, desperate, they tried to interrogate the monkey. The monkey seemed to respond to their questions with gestures. Seeing that it was trying to communicate, they started asking questions. The police inspector asked, "What were the people doing on the bus?" The monkey shook his head in a condemning manner and starts dancing around; he obviously meant that the people were dancing and having fun. The inspector asked, "Hmm, OK, but what else were they doing?" The monkey moved his hand to his mouth as if holding a bottle. The chief says, "Oh! They were drinking, eh?" The inspector continued, "Were they doing anything else?" The monkey nodded his head and moved his arms back and forth, indicating that they were having sex. "If they were having such a great time," asked the inspector, "who was driving the damn bus?"

The monkey cheerfully swung his arms by his sides, as if grabbing a wheel...

****

Why does the Easter bunny hide his eggs? He doesn't want anyone to know he's screwing a chicken!

****

Two rabbits escape from the laboratory and see grass for the first time. They're bouncing through the grass when they meet an older rabbit. "Hello," says the older rabbit. "Would you like to come and stay at my warren?" "What's a warren?" ask the two rabbits. "Don't worry," replies the older rabbit. "Come and see." So off they go. They like the tunnels and chambers of the older rabbit's warren, and decide to stay. In the morning, the two rabbits are awaken by the thumping of the older rabbit. "Come on out for the cabbages," calls the older rabbit. "What's a cabbage?" ask the two rabbits. "Don't worry," replies the older rabbit. "Come and see." So off they go, and they enjoy a day in the fields, eating cabbages. They return very satisfied, with their tummies full of cabbage, and agree a good day was had by all. The following day it's, "Come on out for the cabbages" again, and the same for the day after that. At the end of the third day Rabbit 23 says to Rabbit 17, "These cabbages are good but there must be more to life. Let's go and find it." Rabbit 17 agrees, so off they go, across the grass. They meet a younger rabbit. "Hello," says the younger rabbit. "Come and live in my warren. I've got lots of young girly rabbits staying, and I could use some help." "Girly rabbits?" they ask. "Don't worry," replies the younger rabbit. "Come and see." So they agree, and for three days it's thump-thump-thump. At the end of the third day Rabbit 23 says to Rabbit 17, "It's no good: I've got to get out of here." "Why?" asks Rabbit 17. "This is the best time of our lives!" he exclaims. "Yes," agrees Rabbit 23, "but it's been a week and I'm dying for a fag."

****

Why do Scotsmen wear kilts? So the sheep won't hear the zip.

****

Two shepherds are flying their flock to a new farm. Suddenly the engine fails and the plane begins to plunge quickly to the ground. "Quick!" shouts one, "Grab a parachute and jump!" The other one blinks. "What about the sheep?" The first shepherd stares at him. "Eh? Fuck the sheep!" The second one pauses for a moment, then asks him "Do you think we have time?"

A cowboy goes out to seek his fortune on the frontier of the Old West. He finally settles on a ranching town near the edge of civilisation. It's so near the edge, in fact, that there aren't any women to be found, not for love nor money. Well, he's young and full of hormones, and after a month or so he starts getting randy, so he goes to the saloon to ask around. After a couple of nervous, whispered conversations, it comes out that everybody uses the sheep. He isn't particularly happy about this, but he's really desperate. He buys a bottle to provide some Dutch courage, goes and finds the nearest flock and decides that if he's going to do it at all, he's going to do it right. He spends most of the afternoon picking out the prettiest sheep in the flock. He shampoos her, ties ribbons around her neck and even puts a little bell on her collar. He's also getting pretty drunk. By evening he's finished cleaning up the sheep, and he's not thinking particularly clearly. He's so proud of the way the sheep looks, he decides to take her in to town to show her off at the saloon. When he walks in with the sheep, the room goes quiet. Everybody stares at him. They're not just staring either, but recoiling in shock and horror. He's mortally ashamed, but he's very drunk, so he slurs out, "Whassamada? I thought ever'body went out to the sheep?" Finally, one old timer pipes up. "Yeah, boy, but you got the sheriff's girl."

****

Why do Welsh sheep farmers like to screw sheep on the edge of cliffs? Because they scrabble backwards so charmingly.

****

A young man is on holiday in Wales and starts talking to an old man from the village outside the pub. Trying to be friendly, he asks the old man what his name is, but the old boy gets very irate at this point and says, "Do you see that line of houses over there? I built them all, with my own hands, but do they call me Jones the Builder? Do they buggery! And you see those railway lines over there, now? I laid them all myself, but do they call me Jones the Train? Never! And you see those bridges over that river? I built all of them, too, look you, but do they call me Jones the Bridge? No, boyo, they do not! But, a long, long time ago, when I was young, foolish and drunk, I fucked one sheep..."

Down the Local

2

Jokes about Boozers

So this baby seal walks into a club... Fucking tragedy.

****

A duck walks into a bar and says, "Got any bread?" And the barman says, "No." And the duck says, "Got any bread?" And the barman says, "No." "Got any bread?" "I said N-O, NO." "Got any bread?" "For cryin' out loud – N-O spells NO and I mean NO!" "Got any bread?" "NO, NO, NO, NO, NO, NO, NO, NO, NO, NO, NO!!!" "Got any bread?" "Look, if you ask me one more time if I've got any bread, I'm going to nail your fucking beak to the fucking bar!!" "Got any nails?" "No!" "Got any bread?"

****

An Indian walks into a saloon dressed like a cowboy. He goes up to the bar, looks at the landlord and says, " Me wantum beer." So the landlord gives him a beer. He drinks it. He then goes into the bathroom, pulls out his rifle, shoots the toilet, walks back out, grabs his bag, opens it, pulls out a mangy-looking cat and takes a big bite out of it. The landlord looks at him and says, "Son, what the Sam Hill are you doing?" The Indian replies, "Me being like the white man. Me drink beer, shoot shit and eat pussy."

A bloke walked into the pub and said, "Give me three shots, one each for my best friends and one for me." All through the following month, the bloke drank there in the same way - each time he had three shots, one each for his best friends and one for him. One day he went in and only ordered two shots. The landlord looked sympathetic and said, "What's up, did one of your friends pass away?" "Oh, no," the man replied, "the doctor made me give up drinking."

****

Two fat blokes in a pub, one says to the other "your round." The other one says, "So are you, you fat bastard."

****

Two cannibals walked into a pub and sat down beside a clown. Suddenly the first cannibal whipped out his hunting knife, stabbed the clown through the heart and proceeded to butcher him on the spot. He then cut off a couple of big chunks, handed one to his mate and they both started eating. Suddenly the second cannibal looks up at his friend and says, "Wait a moment. Do you taste something funny?"

****

Two blokes go into a pub to check out the local talent. The first one looks around, and says "Wow, look at the blonde over there in the crop-top. I bet she's really wild in the sack." He goes over to her and starts to make small-talk. Before long, the two of them are heading off out back to her place for a quick shag. The two blokes meet up again the next night in the same bar, and sure enough the blonde is there again. "She's really up for it," says the first one, "Why don't you go give it a shot?" Well, the second bloke goes over and pinches her ass; they start chatting, and five minutes later they're out the back of the pub. When he gets back after 20 minutes or so, he goes over to compare notes with his mate. "So, what do you think? I reckon my wife is better," says the first bloke. "Yeah," says the second bloke, "your wife is better."

****

A baby seal walks into a bar and sits down. "What can I get you?" asks the landlord. "Anything but a Canadian Club," replies the seal.

****

This rural bloke goes into his local one afternoon and to his amazement spots a pair of absolutely stunning babes sitting in one corner of the pub. He goes up to the bar, calls the landlord over and nodding at the girls says, "Keith boy, you'd best tell me what it is they're drinking, 'cos I'm going to get them another one." The landlord gives him a funny look, and says, "Well, I don't know if that's such a good idea, Tom. They're lesbians, see." Tom looks blank. "Lesbians? What's that, then?" The landlord shakes his head and says, "Tell you what, why don't you go ask them?" So Tom shrugs, strolls over to the girls and says, "Well now, forgive my ignorance, but old Keith over at the bar tells me you two are lesbians. What does that mean?" They both smile, and one says, in a slow, sexy drawl, "Well, it means that we like to fuck girls. We like to kiss and stroke each other, suck each other's nipples, finger each other and lick each other's pussies." Tom nods, smiling broadly, and calls to the landlord, "Keith lad, three drinks over here for us lesbians!"

****

A skeleton walks into a pub one night and plops down on a stool. The landlord asks "What can I get you?" The skeleton says, "I'll have a beer, thanks." The landlord passes him a beer and asks "Anything else?" The skeleton nods. "Yeah...a mop..."

****

A man was trying to get into a town centre pub, but the doorman stopped him saying, "Sorry mate, you can't get in here unless you're wearing a tie." The man said, "Okay, I'll be right back," and popped back to his car to find something to use. All he could find, sadly, was a set of jump leads, so he tied them around his neck, went back, and asked, "How's this?" "Well," replied the doorman doubtfully, "Okay, I guess that'll do, but I'm warning you now, don't start anything."

★★★★

A snake slithers into a pub and up to the bar. The landlord says, "I'm sorry, but I can't serve you." "What? Why not?" asks the snake. "Because," says the landlord, "you can't hold your booze."

★★★★

A man went into a small Yorkshire pub and ordered a beer. The landlord served him, and then turned to the news on the TV. Tony Blair was busy giving yet another speech. "God, not that horse's arse again!" said the man. The landlord immediately leaped over the bar and punched the man so hard he knocked him clean off the bar stool. "Look, sorry," said the man, "I didn't know I was in Blair country." The landlord said, "Watch it, lad. You're not in Blair country...You're in horse country."

★★★★

A circus-owner walks into a pub to see everyone crowded around a table watching a little show. On the table is an upside-down pot, and a duck tap-dancing on it. The circus-owner is so impressed that he immediately offers to buy the duck from its owner. After some haggling, they settle on £5,000 for the duck and the pot. Three days later the circus-owner comes back to the pub, furious. He goes up to the bloke he bought the duck from and says: "Your duck is a bloody rip-off! I stuck him on the pot before a whole audience, and he didn't dance a single step!" The bloke looks unimpressed. "Well," he asks, "did you remember to light the candle under the pot?"

****

What's the difference between an Irish wedding and an Irish funeral? There's one fewer drunk at the funeral.

****

A white Texan, a black Texan and a Mexican are walking along a beach. The Mexican spots an old oil lamp, picks it up and rubs it. A genie immediately appears and says that since there are three of them, they can each have one wish. The black Texan thinks for a bit and says, "I wish that my brothers and sisters world-wide were all free of American oppression and back in our ancestral homelands, living happy, successful, wealthy, contented lives." The genie grants his wish, and the black guy vanishes. The Mexican says, "Yeah, that would be nice," so he makes the same wish, but for all Latin Americans, and he too vanishes. The genie then turns to the white Texan, and asks if he too wants freedom and contentment for himself and his fellow-Caucasians. He looks around slowly, grins, and says "Nope. Reckon I'll just have me a beer, boy. It don't get much better than this..."

****

Two tubs of yoghurt walk into a pub. The landlord - himself a tub of cottage cheese - says, "Get out. We don't serve your kind in here." One of the yoghurt cartons looks at him and says, "Why not? We're cultured individuals!"

****

One day, after striking a rich seam of gold in Alaska, a miner came down from the mountains and walked into the nearest saloon in the nearest town. "Ah'm a-lookin' for the meanest, roughest, toughest whore in the Yukon!" he said to the barman. "Well, we got her!" replied the barkeep. "She's upstairs, second room on the right." The miner handed the landlord a gold nugget to pay for two beers and the whore. He grabbed the bottles, stomped up the stairs, kicked open the second door on the right and yelled, "Ah'm a lookin' for the meanest, roughest, toughest whore in the Yukon!" The woman inside the room looked at the miner and said, "Honey, you just found her!" Then she stripped naked, turned her back on the guy, bent over and grabbed her ankles. "Hey, hold on a minute!" said the miner, "I should get to say how we screw." "Relax, sugar, you will," replied the whore, "but I thought you might like to open those beers first."

****

An English bloke, an Irish bloke and a Scots bloke went into a pub for a beer. When the pints rolled up, each one had a fly floating in the top. "Bloody hell!" said the English bloke, disgusted, "That's a bit much. Pour me another one, landlord." The Irish bloke shrugged, said, "Ah, stop making such a fuss, you big lemon," to the English bloke, "Sure now and it's only a little fly," and took a hearty swing. The Scots bloke was horrified. He snatched the fly out of his pint, shook it really hard and yelled, "Spit that oot, ye wee bastard! G'wan, spit it oot or ye'll be sorry!"

****

Yesterday scientists in Canada announced that beer contains small traces of female hormones. To prove the theory, they fed 100 men 12 pints of beer and observed that 100% of them started talking nonsense and lost the ability to drive.

****

A man's disembodied head floats into a pub and orders a pint of beer. When it is served he uses his long tongue to lap up all the beer. No sooner has he finished than his torso appears. He orders another drink, laps it up, and suddenly he has legs, too. "This is great," he says to the landlord, "Give me another drink and we'll see if I can get my arms back, so that I can reach into my trousers, fetch my wallet and pay you." The landlord pours him another one and he laps that one up too. Next thing the landlord knows he's completely vanished. A bloke at the end of the bar turns to the landlord and says, "He should have quit while he was a head."

A fly goes into a pub and orders a drink. The customer on the next stool glances at him and says to the landlord, "What's with him?" The landlord says, "Oh, he works in the restaurant down the street." The man says to the fly, "That's fascinating. What kind of work do you do?" The fly sighs, "They put me in bowls of soup. It's tough on my health."

****

What's the difference between a Irish woman and an Irish goddess? About five pints.

****

A man walks into a bar – he sits down and orders a drink. The bar man gives him his drink, accompanied by a bowl of peanuts. To his surprise a voice comes from the peanut bowl. "You look great tonight!" it said, "You really look fantastic... and that aftershave is just wonderful!" The man is obviously a little confused, but tries to ignore it. Realising he has no cigarettes he wanders over to the cigarette machine. After inserting his money, another voice comes from the machine. "You WANKER... Oh my god you STINK... Do you know, you're almost as ugly as your mother." By now, the man is extremely perplexed. He turns to the barman for an explanation. "Ah yes sir," the barman responds, "The peanuts are complimentary, but the cigarette machine is out of order."

****

Descartes walks into a pub. "Would you like a beer, sir?" asks the landlord politely. Descartes replies, "I think not" and ping! he vanishes.

****

This bloke walks into a pub and there's a horse behind the bar serving the drinks. The bloke stares at the horse in amazement, so the horse says, "Look, what are you staring at, mate? Haven't you ever seen a horse serving drinks before?" The bloke says, "No, it's not that...it's just that I never dreamed that the parrot would sell the place."

****

John met Lisa down the pub one night and began buying her drinks. They got on pretty well together, and John suggested they go to his flat for a little light entertainment. Well it wasn't long before they found themselves in bed screwing passionately. As they were making love, John noticed that Lisa's toes curled up whenever he thrust into her particularly firmly. When they were done John laid back on the bed and said, "I must have been pretty good tonight. I noticed your toes curling up when I was going deep." Lisa looked over at him and smiled. "That usually happens when someone forgets to remove my tights."

****

Have you heard the new pickup line currently in fashion at gay bars? "Excuse me, can I push your stool up for you?"

****

A drunk bloke staggers into a pub, bumping into customers and spilling drinks as he makes his way to the bar. "Get the fuck out of here!" shouts the landlord when the drunk bloke finally makes it over. "I've gotta use the bog," slurs the drunk. "Fuck off right this instant or I'll throw you out myself," yells the landlord. "I gotta use the bog," says the drunk bloke again and starts to unbutton his trousers. "For fuck's sake! Hold on, hold on," says the landlord. "Alright, you can go to the toilet, but afterwards you piss off!" The drunk agrees and stumbles off to the toilet. After about five minutes a loud scream rips through the crowded bar, and everyone goes absolutely silent. Suddenly there's another loud scream. The landlord and a couple of regulars sprint to the bathroom to find out what's going on. When they get there, they find the drunk sitting down in the corner. "What the fuck is going on?" asks the landlord. "Look, 's your bog. I've had a pony, and every time I try to flush it crushes my balls!" says the drunk. "You stupid wanker!" screams the landlord, "You've crapped in my mop bucket!"

****

A bloke opens a bar, but he's having difficulty thinking of a name for it. "Name it after something you remember happily," a friend tells him; so remembering an old girlfriend of his he calls it "Lucy's Legs". A couple of weeks later, three blokes are waiting outside the bar for opening time. A policemen walks up to them, and curiously asks "Everything alright, gentlemen?" One of the blokes turns round to him and says, "Yes, thanks, officer. We're just waiting for Lucy's Legs to open so we can pop in and get a bite to eat."

****

A cowboy walked into a bar, dressed entirely in paper. It wasn't long before he was arrested for rustling.

****

A bloke was watching the football, drinking a few tinnies and popping peanuts into his mouth, when his wife called him from the kitchen. He turned his head towards her and accidentally popped a peanut into his ear. Well, they both tried and tried but neither could get it out. "Alright then," she said, "We'd better get you to hospital." As they walked out, their teenage daughter and her boyfriend came up and the daughter asked, "Where are you and dad going, mum?" The mother replied, "Oh, we're just off to the hospital. Your father has a peanut stuck in his ear." The boyfriend then said, "I tell you what; before you go, let me try to dislodge it." They agreed, so the lad stuck two fingers up the father's nose and told him to blow. The father blew, and out popped the peanut. As they headed back inside, the mother turned to her husband and said, "That lad's pretty clever. What do you think he'll be when he grows up?" The father replied, "By the smell of his fingers, he'll be our son-in-law."

****

Three blokes are driving around, necking beers and having a laugh when the driver looks in the mirror and sees the flashing lights of a police car telling him to pull over. The other two are really worried. "What are we going to do with our beers? We're in trouble!" "No," the driver says, "it's OK, just pull the label off of your bottle like this and stick it on your forehead. Let me do the talking." So they all pull the labels off their bottles and stick them to their foreheads, and the bloke pulls over. The policeman then walks up and says, "You lads were swerving all around the road back there. Have you been drinking?" "Oh, no, officer," says the driver, pointing to his forehead, "We're trying to give up, so we're on the patch."

****

A bloke walks into a pub with a pet crocodile at his side. He puts the crocodile up on the bar, turns to the astonished customers and says, "I'll do you a deal. I'll open this crocodile's mouth and place my dick inside it. The croc will close his mouth for one minute. He'll then open his mouth, and I'll remove my dick unscathed. In return for witnessing this feat, each of you will buy me a beer." The crowd nodded their agreement. The man got up on the bar, dropped his trousers, and placed his dick in the crocodile's open mouth. The croc closed his mouth, and the crowd winced in sympathy for the guy. After a minute, the bloke grabbed a beer bottle and rapped the crocodile hard on the top of its head. The croc opened his mouth, and the man removed his dick unscathed, as promised. The crowd cheered, and the first of his free beers was delivered. A couple of minutes later, the bloke stood up again and made another offer. "There's fifty quid here waiting for anyone else who's willing to give it a try." A hush fell over the crowd, and everyone shuffled their feet. After a while, a hand went up at the back of the crowd and a woman timidly called out. "Well, I'll try, but you have to promise not to hit me on the head with that beer bottle."

✳✳✳✳

A bloke walks into a pub and orders a double whisky. He pays up, gulps it down and looks into his shirt pocket. He then orders another double, pays, gulps it down and look into his shirt pocket again. He orders a third drink and does the same thing. After the sixth double, he gets up and starts to stagger out. Curiosity gets the better of the landlord, and he says to the bloke, "Excuse me, but I noticed that every time you had a drink, you looked inside your pocket. I was wondering what's in there." The blokes looks at him for a moment, then slurs, "Well, I keep a picture of my wife in that pocket. Every time I have a drink, I take a look. When she starts looking good, I go home."

✳✳✳✳

An obviously drunk bloke staggers into a pub and seats himself at the bar. After being served, he notices a woman sitting a few stools down. He motions the landlord over and says "Landlord, I'd like to buy that old douchebag down there a drink." Somewhat offended, the landlord replies, "Sir, I run a respectable establishment, and I don't appreciate you calling my female customers douchebags." The man looks ashamed for a moment and says "Yes, you're right, that was uncalled-for...please allow me to buy the woman a cocktail." "That's better," says the landlord, and he goes over to the woman. "Madam, the gentleman at the bar there would like to buy you a drink. What would you like?" "How nice!" replied the woman, "I'll have a vinegar and water, thanks."

****

One night a policeman was staking out a particularly notorious pub for drunk drivers. Towards closing time he saw a bloke stumble out of the pub, trip on the kerb and try his keys in five different cars before his own. Then he sat in the front seat of his car fumbling with his keys for several minutes. The policeman sat and waited for him to start up, then almost as soon as the man had left the car park he pulled the guy over and gave him a breathalyser test. After asking a few pointless questions and fumbling with the device for a minute or two, he blew into the box. The results showed no alcohol at all. Puzzled, the policeman made the driver repeat the test, and got the same result again - the bloke was sober. Worried, the policeman offered to fetch medical assistance if the driver was ill. The chap just smiled at him and said "Everything is fine, officer. I'm tonight's designated decoy!"

****

A dishevelled man, stinking like a distillery, flopped onto a bar stool next to the local Catholic vicar. His tie was tattered, his face was covered with lipstick prints and a half-empty bottle of gin was sticking out of his coat pocket. He pulled a newspaper out of his coat and began reading. After a few minutes, the dishevelled bloke turned to the vicar and asked, "Tell me Father, what causes arthritis?" The priest looked at the chap for a moment or two, and then disapprovingly said: "Actually, it's caused by loose morals, cavorting with cheap, wicked women, drinking excessive quantities of alcohol and having contempt for your fellows." "Well, I'll be damned," the drunk muttered, returning to his paper. The vicar thought about what he had said for a few moments, then nudged the man and apologised. "I'm sorry, I didn't mean to be so heavy with you. How long have you had arthritis?" The dishevelled bloke shook his head, and said, "I don't have arthritis, Father. I was just reading here that the Pope does."

****

After a major beer festival, the biggest brewery presidents decided to go out for a beer together. They picked a well-stocked pub and went in. The guy from Corona goes up to the bar and says, "Hey, señor, I would like the world's best beer, a Corona." The landlord takes a bottle from the shelf and hands it to him. The bloke from Budweiser says, "Give me the King Of Beers, a Budweiser." The landlord passes him one. The chap from Coors says, "I'd like the only beer made with Rocky Mountain spring water; give me a Coors." He gets it. The bloke from Guinness sits down and says, "Oh, give me a Coke." The landlord is a little surprised, but gives him what he ordered. The other presidents look over at him and ask, "What's up, why aren't you drinking Guinness?" The Guinness guy shrugs and replies, "Well, I decided if you lot weren't going to drink beer, neither would I."

****

A middle-aged woman and her husband visit a disco, just to remember what it used to be like. After a few dances they sit down at the side to recuperate. A few minutes later a bloke comes over and asks the woman to dance. She is flattered and, with an approving glance from her husband, accepts the invitation. Well, after a few minutes bopping, the bloke leans over to her and says, "You know, I think you're really good-looking. Could I kiss you, please?" The woman is a bit bowled over but replies, "Certainly not - I'm a married woman and my husband is over there." The dancing continues, and after another few minutes the man leans over again and says, "I really do think that you're the most attractive woman I've seen for ages. Could I fondle your tits, please?" This time the woman is shocked, and she replies, "No! What sort of person do you think I am?" The bloke apologises, makes the peace and they continue dancing. After a little while more the bloke leans over for a third time and says, "I think you're so lovely that I'd like to turn you upside down, fill you with beer and drink it out of you." The woman is horrified, slaps the bloke in the face and goes back to her husband. "Do you know what that man wanted to do to me?" she asks him. "He wanted to kiss me." "What?" exclaims her husband. "That's not all either; he wanted to feel my tits too," she continues. Her husband gets up and asks "Where is he? I'll show him. I'll knock his block off!" "There's more," said his wife. "He wanted to turn me upside down, fill me with beer and drink it out of me." Her husband immediately sat down again. "What are you sitting down for?" she asked, "I thought you were going to go and sort him out?" "You must be joking," her husband replied. "I'm not messing with anyone who can drink 16 pints in one go!"

****

A small bloke is standing by the bar when he looks up and notices a really huge guy standing next to him. The huge guy glances down, sees the small bloke looking up at him and booms out "Turner Brown, seven feet tall, 350 pounds, with a 20-inch dick, a three-pound left testicle and a three-pound right testicle." The small bloke faints dead away. Concerned, the big guy picks the little one up, shakes him gently and brings him back to consciousness. "What's wrong with you?" he asks. The small bloke says faintly, "Look, what did you say?" The big guy shrugs and repeats, "Turner Brown, seven feet tall, 350 pounds, with a 20-inch dick, a three-pound left testicle and a three-pound right testicle." The small bloke says, "Thank God! I thought you said 'Turn around'."

****

A herd of buffalo can only move as fast as the slowest buffalo, so it follows that the brain can only operate as fast as the slowest brain cells. The slowest buffalo are the sick and weak ones so they die off first, making it possible for the herd to move at a faster pace. Like the buffalo, the weak, slow brain cells are the ones that are killed off first by excessive drinking and partying. This makes your brain operate faster...

****

An Irishman's been at a pub all night, drinking. The landlord finally says that the bar is closed, so he stands up to leave and falls flat on his face. He decides to crawl outside and get some fresh air, in the hope that it will sober him up. Once outside, he tries to stand up again and falls flat on his face again. So the Irishman crawls home. At the door he tries to stand up yet again, only to fall flat on his face once more, so he crawls through the door and up the stairs. When he reaches his bedroom, he tries one final time to stand up. This time he collapses right on to the bed and, exhausted, falls fast asleep. When he wakes up the next morning, his wife is standing over him yelling, "You've been out drinking again!" "How did you know?" he asks. "The pub called, you stupid eejit. You left your wheelchair there again."

****

A bloke walks into a pub and orders ten shots of vodka, no ice. As the landlord hands them over he crashes them down, one after the other. "Are you alright?" asks the landlord, "Why are you drinking so fast?" The bloke replies, "You'd understand if you knew what I had in my pocket." Thoroughly perplexed, the landlord asks "So what do you have in your pocket?" The bloke grimaces and says, "A grand total of 25p."

****

This bloke walks into a bar at the top of a very tall building. He sits down, orders a huge beer, knocks it back, walks over to the window and jumps out. Five minutes later, he walks into the bar again, orders another huge beer, necks it, walks over to the window and jumps out again. Another five minutes pass, he reappears and repeats the whole thing, and so it continues. About half an hour later, another guy at the bar stops the first bloke and says, "Hey, how the hell are you doing that?" The first bloke replies, "Oh, it's really simple physics. When you knock back the beer quickly it makes you all warm inside, and since warm air rises, if you just hold your breath you become lighter than air and float down to the sidewalk." "Wow!" exclaims the second man, "I've got to give that a go!" So he orders a huge beer, downs it, goes to the window, jumps out and plummets to land with a splat on the pavement below. The landlord looks over at the first bloke and says, "Superman, you're an asshole when you're drunk."

****

A Mexican, an Irishman, an African, a kilted Scotsman, a priest, two lesbians, a rabbi and a nun walk into a bar. The landlord looks up and says, "What the hell is this? Some kind of joke?"

****

An Indian scout was checking the area on behalf of some buffalo hunters, searching for the herds. He put his ear to the ground. "Ugg", he said, "Deer come!" The hunters looked at him with awe. "How the heck can you tell that?" asked one. The scout answered, "Simple. Ear sticky."

****

A bloke walks into a pub with a yellow, long-nosed, short-legged dog under his arm. "That's one ugly dog," says another patron, petting his Doberman. "Heh," says the bloke, "that he is, but he's a mean little bastard." "Is that so?" asks the other patron, "I'll bet you £50 my dog will kick his arse in less than two minutes." The bloke agrees, so they put their dogs face to face and each gives the command to attack. In the twinkling of an eye, the little yellow dog has bitten the Doberman clean in half. "Fuck!" shouts the Doberman's devastated owner, "He killed Fang! What kind of damn dog is this?" "Well," says the bloke, "before I cut off his tail and painted him yellow he was a crocodile."

****

A guy is having a drink in a very dark bar. He leans over to a large woman next to him and says, "Do you wanna hear a funny blonde joke?" The big woman replies, "Well, before you tell that joke, you should know something. I'm blonde, six feet tall, 210 lb., and I'm a professional triathlete and bodybuilder. The blonde woman sitting next to me is 6' 2", weighs 220 lb., and she's an ex-professional wrestler. Next to her is a blonde who's 6' 5", weighs 250 lb., and she's a current professional kick boxer. Now, do you still want to tell that blonde joke?" The guy thinks about it a second and says, "No, not if I'm going to have to explain it three times."

****

Two blokes decided to open a real ale brewery in the foothills. After several months of careful work, they produced a product with a golden straw-like colour and a good strong flavour of hops. They sent it to the chemical lab at the MAFF for testing, and after waiting impatiently for three weeks, the lab analysis came back. It read, "Dear Sirs, Our analysis of the sample sent to us indicates that your horse has diabetes."

****

A Jew and a Chinese guy were sitting at a bar drinking. All of a sudden the Jew turned and punched the Chinese guy in the face, knocking him off his stool. Stunned, the Chinese guy got up and said, "What the hell was that for?" The Jew replied, "That was for Pearl

Harbour." The Chinese guy said, "That was the Japanese. I'm Chinese." The Jew says, "Well, you have black hair, slitty eyes and buck teeth. It's all the same to me." The Chinese guy says "Okay," sits on his stool and continues drinking. About a minute later the Chinese guy turns round and punches the Jew in the face, knocking him off his stool. The Jew gets up and says, "That had better not be for me hitting you before." The Chinese guy says, "No, that was for the Titanic." The Jew replies, "The Titanic? That was an iceberg." The Chinese guy looks coolly at the Jew and says, "Iceberg, Goldberg, it's all the same to me..."

****

A woman walked into a bar carrying a duck under her arm. "Get that dog out of here!" yelled the landlord. "That's not a dog, stupid!" she replied, "That's a duck!" "I wasn't talking to you!" said the landlord.

****

Two drunkards were sitting at the bar. One was crying. The other asked him what was wrong. "I've puked all over myself again, and my wife is going to leave me this time; she warned me about it." The other drunk said "Do what I do, pal. Explain to your wife that some other guy puked on you. Put a tenner in your shirt pocket, and tell her that he was sorry and gave you the cash to get your clothes cleaned." "Sounds like a great idea," said the first drunk. When he got home, his wife was furious and started shouting at him about his clothes, how disgusting he was and that she'd had enough; she was off. The drunk started telling his lie, saying: "Look for yourself; there's the money in my shirt pocket." His wife looked in the pocket and found twenty quid. "Hang on a minute," she said suspiciously, "I thought you said the bloke gave you ten pounds for puking on you, not 20." The drunk nods, "Yeah, he did, but he crapped in my pants too."

****

A bloke bounced into the pub grinning and said to the landlord, "The beers are on me! My wife just ran away with my best friend." The landlord smiled and said, "Well, that's a shame. How come you aren't sad?" "Sad?" replied the bloke, "They've saved me a fortune! They were both pregnant!"

****

This bloke walked into a pub with a large toad on his head. "Where the hell did you get that?" asked the barman. "Well," the toad replied, "You won't believe it, but it started out as a little wart on my arse!"

****

A bloke is in the toilet of his local pub taking a slash. He looks around, and notices this black guy also using the urinals, and he's got a huge cock. "Damn!" says the bloke, in awe, "I wish I had a cock like that." The black guy looks over at him, "Well, it's simple. All you have to do is whack your dick on the side of your bath tub every morning." "Really?" asks the bloke. "Really," answers the black guy. The following week the black guy sees the bloke in the pub again, so he walks over and says to him, "So, have you been following my advice?" The bloke nods. "Well," says the black guy, "I can't help you with the size, but at least you've got the colour right!"

****

A fish staggers into a bar. "What can I get you?" asks the landlord. The fish croaks "Water..."

****

A man walks into a butcher shop and asks the butcher "Are you a gambling man?" "I am" replies the butcher. "OK" says the man, "I bet you can't reach up and touch that meat hanging from those hooks." "I'm not doing that" replies the butcher. "I thought you said you were a gambling man?" "I am – but the steaks are too high."

****

The Lone Ranger rides into town during the hottest part of summer. He stops outside a saloon and tells Tonto to run in circles around

Silver, waving his poncho to keep a nice breeze on the horse while he goes in for a drink. A couple of minutes later, a man dressed in black swaggers into the bar and says, "You the Lone Ranger?" "Yes, I am," the Lone Ranger replies. "Well," says the man in black, "Did ya know ya left your injun runnin'?"

****

A dark-haired woman was sitting in a pub, wearing a tube top. She never shaved her armpits so, as a result, she had a thick black bush under each arm. Every 20 minutes, she raised her arm to signal the landlord to pour her another drink. This went on all evening. Towards the end of the night, a drunk at the end of the bar pointed at her and said to the landlord, "Hey, I'd like to buy the ballerina a drink. What's she drinking?" The landlord replied, "She's no ballerina." The drunk said, "Come off it. Any girl that can lift her leg that high has to be a ballerina!"

****

A bloke stumbles home completely plastered. He spends an hour trying to get the key into the lock, with no success, when a policeman happens to pass by. "Is everything alright, sir?" asks the policeman. "I can't get the damn key in the lock, officer," slurs the man. The policeman helps him out with the key and starts to go on his way. "Wait, wait," shouts the drunk, "I really appreciate it. Let me show you my house!" "No, thank you, sir, I'll just be on my way," says the policeman. "I insist," presses the drunk, "It'll only take a second, and I really want to show you!" So the policeman agrees, to keep the peace, and they go inside. They enter the living room. "There's my TV, my stereo, and all that," says the man. "That's nice," the policeman replies. They go through to the kitchen. "There's my microwave, the new refrigerator...pretty nice, eh?" says the man. "Lovely," replies the policeman. Into the kids' bedroom: "Those are my two baby boys." "Yes, they look cute." Finally they get through to the man's bedroom. "And that's my wife, and that's me next to her."

****

This American redneck walks into a bar and says, "Gimme a Coke." The landlord says "Nah, you want a beer, mate. Every night you come in, have three beers and leave." The redneck says "Yeah, but last night I had three beers here, then I went to the bar down the street and had ten more beers. Then I went home and blew chunks." The landlord says, "Well, don't worry, it happens to the best of us." The redneck says, "You don't understand. Chunks is my pit-bull!"

****

Three blokes are sitting with their dogs in a pub by a nice log fire, and they get talking about them. The first one says "My dog is called Woodworker...Go, Woodworker! At 'im, boy." The dog immediately grabs a log from the fire with his teeth and uses his claws to fashion a beautiful wooden figurine. The next one says, "My dog is called Stoneworker...Go, Stoneworker! Come by, lad!" The dog drags a stone from the fireplace, goes at it and a beautiful carving emerges. The third one looks at the other two and says, "Well, my dog is called Ironworker." He puts the tongs into the fire and leaves them until they get red-hot. "Now," he says, picking up the hot tongs, "I'll just slap him on the bollocks with these, and you watch him make a bolt for the door."

****

A Scots chap in England is walking home pissed from the pub, as usual, and decides to take a quick nap on a nearby bench, to provide stamina for the rest of the journey. While he's dozing, a couple of girls stroll by. One says to the other, "Hey, is it true that they don't wear anything beneath those kilts?" The other giggles and says, "Let's take a look". So, after finding that the chap is indeed naked under his kilt, the first one says, "We should leave something to let him know we were here." So saying, she removes a blue ribbon from her hair and carefully ties it around his bell-end. When he comes round a couple of hours later, the Scot nips behind a bush to relieve himself. He finds the ribbon, and in tones of awe murmurs, "I don't know where you've been, laddie, but I see you took first prize..."

Two vampires walked into a bar and called for the landlord. "I'll have a glass of blood," said one. "I'll have a glass of plasma," said the other. "Okay," replied the landlord, "that'll be one blood and one blood lite."

****

This bloke walks into a pub and orders a beer. The barman looks at the bloke and says, "Have you seen Eileen?" The bloke is rather confused and asks, "Eileen who?" The landlord replies, "How about I lean over and you kiss my hairy arse?" The man is fairly offended by this, and walks out of the door and into the bar across the street, where he sits down and orders a beer. While he is drinking his beer, he tells the landlord what the other barman said to him. The landlord says, "You know, what you should do is go back over there and ask him if he has seen Ben, and when he says 'Ben who?' you say 'How about I bend over and you kiss my hairy arse?'" So the bloke goes back across the street, and asks the barman if he has seen Ben. The barman immediately replies, "Yep, he just went out the door with Eileen." The bloke looks puzzled for a moment, then asks "Eileen who...?"

****

A bloke goes into a pub and orders five doubles. The landlord asks him, "Jesus, are you okay?" The bloke answers, "I just found out my brother is gay." The landlord nods sympathetically and pours the drinks; the guy downs them, pays up and leaves. The same bloke returns a week later, and this time he orders ten doubles. The landlord again asks him, "Are you okay?" The bloke shakes his head. "I just found out my other brother is gay, too." Well, the landlord pours, and the bloke drinks up. The next week, he goes back into the bar and orders 15 doubles. "Shit! Doesn't anyone at all in your family like girls apart from you?" the landlord asks. "Yes," replies the bloke dolefully, "my kid sister."

The Devil walks into a crowded bar. When the people see who it is, they all run out screaming except this one old man. So the Devil saunters up to him and asks, "Do you know who I am?" The old man sips his beer, looks at the Devil, and answers, "Yup, happen I do." The Devil says, "Well, aren't you afraid of me?" The old man looks him up and down and says, "I've been married to your sister for 47 years. Why the hell should I be scared of you?"

So, this dyslexic walks into a bra...

An Arab has spent many days crossing the desert without finding a source of water. It gets so bad that his camel dies of thirst. He's crawling through the sands, certain that he has breathed his last breath, when all of a sudden he sees a shiny object sticking out of the sand several yards ahead of him. He crawls to the object, pulls it out of the sand, and discovers that it was a Manischevitz wine bottle. It appears that there may be a drop or two left in the bottle, so he unscrews the top and out pops a genie. "Well, kid," says the genie, "You know how it works. You have three wishes." "I'm not going to trust you," says the Arab. "I'm not going to trust a genie!" "What do you have to lose? It looks like you're a goner anyway!" The Arab thinks about this for a minute, and decides that the genie is right. "OK, I wish I were in a lush oasis with plentiful food and drink." ***POOF*** The Arab finds himself in the most beautiful oasis he has ever seen. And he is surrounded with jugs of wine and platters of delicacies. "OK, kid, what's your second wish?" "My second wish is that I were rich beyond my wildest dreams." ***POOF*** The Arab finds himself surrounded by treasure chests filled with rare gold coins and precious gems. "OK, kid, you have just one more wish. Better make it a good one!" After thinking for a few minutes, the Arab says: "I wish I were white and surrounded by beautiful women." ***POOF*** The Arab is turned into a Tampon. The moral of the story is: Be careful of what you wish for. There may be a string attached.

This bloke is really desperate for a shit, so he nips into a nearby crowded pub. He looks around and sees that the toilets are upstairs, so he pops up there. When he gets up to the first floor, though, he can't find the damn things anywhere. Eventually, after several minutes of hunting around, he finds a hole in the floor and decides it's better than dumping on the floor, so he craps into it. When he's finished up, he goes back downstairs thinking he'll have a quick beer. To his amazement, the place is deserted; just the landlord standing behind the bar. "Where is everyone?" he asks. The landlord looks at him in amazement. "Where the hell were you when the shit hit the fan?"

****

An angry wife met her husband at the door. There was alcohol on his breath and lipstick on his collar. "I assume," she snarled, "that there is a very good reason for you to come waltzing in here at six o'clock in the morning?" "There is," he replied. "Breakfast."

****

Our Beer, which art in barrels, hallowed be thy foam. Thy hopdom come, thou will be drunk, at home as it is down the pub. Give us this day our daily beverage, and forgive us our spillages, as we forgive those who spill over us, and lead us not into naughtiness, but deliver us from kebabs, for thine is the taste, the clarity and the head, forever and ever. Amen. That concludes today's service, gentlemen.

Pun Away! Pun Away!

3

Shaggy Dog Stories

There was a bloke who was famous across the world for the quality of the tulips that he grew. People used to come from all around to admire them, and to try and get the secret of how he grew them out of him. He was very cagey, and would only say, "I just put the bulbs in, and they come up perfectly." No one believed him, of course, but no one could discover what it was that he used to turn ordinary bulbs into the most beautiful tulip blooms that had ever been grown. There were whole fields of them, ranks and ranks, all identical and all perfect. Eventually, a friend of his of long standing decided to get the secret out of the tulip-grower and, if it was a simple enough trick, to maybe turn a few quid on the side. He invited his horticultural friend over one evening; they settled down to watch the football and have a few tins of beer, and once the grower started to relax, they moved on to Scotch; eventually, the friend started to gently steer the conversation towards tulips. Well, by now the grower was drunk, and his guard was down. They chatted for a while about tulips, with the friend congratulating the grower on his skill, and eventually, when the friend asked, "So, how do you get them so good, anyway?" he tapped the side of his nose and announced, "Hamsters!" Well, the friend was taken aback, and peered at the grower suspiciously to see if he was taking the piss, but he looked sincere. "Don't be daft," said the friend, "how can hamsters make ordinary tulip bulbs produce flowers the quality of yours?" "Well," said the grower, "On my other plot of land, I breed hamsters. Not just one or two, mind you, but thousands of the little buggers. God! They don't half stink out a place, I can tell you. It's appalling. Anyway, when they become adults I wait until the evening, when they're asleep, then run over them all with a huge turbo-charged steamroller that I got especially for the purpose. It's a beauty — 12,000cc of growling monster, thundering around at 40mph. When they're all accounted for, I bulldoze the mush into a machine which cans them into barrels, which I store in a big warehouse. At the start of the growing season, I go out at night with the old fertilising machine, filled up from the tins of course, and spread the mess all over the fields. Then I then get the tractor out, and plough and plough until it's all thoroughly worked into the ground. The next day I plant the bulbs, and you've seen the results for yourself." The friend paused for a moment and thought it over, then said, "Well I suppose it must work, but I really can't see how!" The tulip-grower grinned at him. "Obvious, isn't it? I copied the idea from the Dutch flower-growers, 'cos they're the real experts when you get down to it. I grow tulips from hamster jam!"

✳✳✳✳

June 3, 1861. Out here, at the frontier, it's very easy to wonder if maybe those old missionaries weren't right all those centuries ago, and I have actually come to the edge of the world. There's no other white man — or woman, damn it — for 100 miles in any direction. I devote my time to reading my copy of the Bible and tending my patch of cucumbers. This outpost was supposed to hold back the Indians, but that's a joke, and it seems to be unnecessary, anyway.

June 11, 1861. I was excited this morning by an interesting, if silent, visitor. One of the Indians from the tribe that lives nearby stood at the top of the hill and watched me perform my chores for over an hour, and then left without a word. Contact with the local natives is a thrilling prospect, and I have resolved to do nothing to scare them away.

June 19, 1861. Breakthrough! I have finally managed to convince the Indians to make proper contact. I taught them the word for "fort", which seemed like a simple enough place to begin. They in turn taught me the Indian word "toitonka", which refers to a mysterious device, a tiny horseless carriage made of metal. I envy these people their simplicity.

June 22, 1861. Today I was greatly flattered to be taken to the Indians' village. It is built on one of the many flat-topped plateaux, or mesas, in the area. As the buffalo herds decline, this noble tribe too will face a decline of its own. They need a fighting chance, so I will try to teach them agriculture. Their name for themselves is "Waatch," which, as far as I can make out, means "The people known as the Waatch" in their language. I am known to them — it seems that they've been observing me closely — as "Stinchapocla" which means "he who has bodily odour."

July 8, 1861. Today I received a rude awakening; I have been foolish. The Indians are in fact fully aware of agriculture, and have nothing to do with the buffalo. That makes sense, I suppose — no nomads would build a village on a mesa. Unfortunately, they are suffering from a drought, as they have no rivers on top of the mesa, and the rainfall has been poor recently. I can help at last! I have told them to dig a ditch from near the stream that runs past my fort, up the cliff, to their mesa-top fields. They seem doubtful, but they are desperate, and their shaman, Bahnee, has told them to go ahead. In the meantime, I am pickling my youngest cucumbers.

July 20, 1861. The drought is getting critical, but the ditch is complete and my pickles are now ready. I have lined the ditch with pickles. The Waatch are nervous, but I have promised them results in the morning.

July 21, 1861. Success! The stream has been diverted, and is flowing up the cliff-face to the Waatch fields. I have gained much status by what they see as a feat of magic. The shaman asked about my powerful medicine, but I came clean and told him that I was simply making use of a common fact in my world. After all, everyone knows that Dill Waters run Steep.

When I was young, I got separated from my parents in a crowd. Well, I was crying and crying, and eventually I found a found a policeman who said he would help. I asked him, "Do you think we'll ever be able to find them?" He replied "I'm not sure, lad. There are so many places to hide..."

****

It's a well-known fact that if you want an improvement in your working conditions, you should always tackle your boss about your issues one at a time. After all, you should never put all your begs in one ask-it.

****

Charlie, a big green frog, hopped into a bank one morning, with a briefcase neatly tucked under his right foreleg. He waited in the queue for a bit, then hopped up to the cashier and leaped onto the counter, sitting down in front of the cashier, Miss Jane Grey. "I need a loan," Charlie announced. Miss Grey, not wanting to seem flustered by meeting a talking frog, paused a moment, then replied, "I'm sorry, sir, but the Northlands Savings Bank doesn't normally issue loans to amphibians." Rapidly flicking open the briefcase, Charlie got out a sheaf of planning permits, schedules, estimates and blueprints. He passed them over to Miss Grey, and said, "Look, I need a loan. I have a sure-fire construction project in mind. Down in the marsh, we're very short of affordable housing. All my relatives need places. I have the permits. Paul, an architect friend of mine — a newt, as it happens — has drawn up the plans. Everything is approved and in order. There's a lot of local interest. All I need now is the financing." For poor Miss Grey, the situation was getting stranger and stranger. It wasn't enough that there was a talking frog sitting just a few inches in front of her, but he was now talking about his architect newt, plans, permits and amphibian interests. On the verge of freaking out completely, she blurted, "I'm terribly sorry, sir, I can't help you. You'll have to see our loan officer, Miss Black. Wait here for a moment please, and I'll get her." Miss Grey was gone for a while. After several minutes of spirited conversation at the other side of the bank, she returned with the loan officer. "Hello, sir," she said, "I'm Patricia Black, the loan officer here. How can I help you?" Charlie repeated his speech again, telling her about his idea, the plans and permits, the housing situation and his friend Paul, the newt architect. Miss Black decided to put an end to the whole nonsense swiftly, so she said, "What do you have to use as collateral for this loan? You must have something of value that you can mortgage to obtain a loan like this." Charlie wasn't the least bit thrown; he dug into his briefcase again. "I have this," he said, and brought out a crystal trinket on a silver chain, "It's extremely valuable". "I can't give you a loan based on that thing!" said Miss Black. "I don't even know what it is!" Well, Charlie begged for a while. He pleaded. Finally, he demanded to see the bank manager. Miss Grey, the cashier, went to go and fetch him when Miss Black reluctantly agreed, and another lively conversation took place at the far side of the bank. The manager eventually came over and asked, "What appears to be the problem, Miss Black?" She looked at him doubtfully, then explained that Charlie wanted to take out a loan, to construct housing in the marsh for his friends and relatives, that he has plans and permits, but all he had for collateral was the trinket. The manager, perplexed by this whole situation, took the trinket from Charlie and had a long, close look at it. Finally, he handed it back to Charlie and nodded thoughtfully, then turned to the loan officer and said, "It's a knick-knack, Patty Black. Give the frog a loan."

****

A little baby bunny rabbit was orphaned. Fortunately for him, a nearby family of squirrels took him in and raised him as if he were one of their own. As you might expect, a squirrelly upbringing produced some peculiar behavioural patterns on the part of the rabbit, including a tendency for him to forget about jumping but rather to run around like his step-brothers and step-sisters. When the rabbit hit puberty, he found himself faced with an identity crisis. What was he? He went to his foster parents to discuss the problem. They talked about how he felt different from his step-brothers and step-sisters, how he was unsure of his place in the universe, and how he was generally forlorn. His squirrel dad's wise response was, "Don't scurry, be hoppy."

There was an organic farmer who didn't want to use a tractor on his small fields, so instead he had a pair of shire-horses to pull his plough and his wagons. Unfortunately a group of small birds had made nests inside the horses' manes, weaving the hairs together, which prevented him from hitching the reins properly. He tried everything he could think of to get rid of the birds, but no matter what he did they just came back again. He tried lotions, potions, shields and notions. He kept the stable colder and he kept the stable warmer. He went to horse doctors, he went to bird specialists, he went to his local MP, he went to the vet, and he even called the MAFF. He trimmed the manes down as much as he could. He tried loud bangs, cats and little horsehair scarecrows. Nothing would make the birds leave his horses' alone. Finally he took advice from a bloke down the pub and went to see a supposed wise woman at the end of the village. The wise woman listened to his story, nodded, and gave him some vile-smelling yeast extract to rub into the manes. To his delight and amazement, it worked. Within two days, all the birds had gone and the horses could get back to work. The farmer was extremely pleased, but puzzled. He went back to the wise woman, and asked her: "Well, you're obviously very wise, but how come your yeast extract was able to solve a problem that nothing, not even vets and bureaucrats hadn't been able to?" She smiled and said, "Ah, it's simple. Yeast is yeast, and nest is nest, and never the mane shall tweet."

Does fuzzy logic tickle your brain?

****

In days of yore, a doughty knight was on a vital quest. The life of the King hung in the balance, for unless he was able to rush a special potion back to the palace that very day the King would surely die. He was still about a hundred miles from the palace when his horse, exhausted from the rate at which the knight was pushing it, became lame. Well, through the woods he could see a small inn, so he ran and ran up to the inn as fast as he could. He headed straight for the stables, found the inn's stable-keeper, and shouted, "I must have a horse! The life of the King hangs in the balance, for he will surely die unless I can get a special potion back to him this very day." The stable-keeper shook his old, grizzled head regretfully, and said, "Ahh, I'm dreadful sorry, Sir Knight. We haven't got any horses in the stable today. Patrons are a bit light on the ground at this point in the season, what with the crops and all." The knight was distraught. "This is disastrous! Oh, evil chance! You must have some steed, good man — a pony, a donkey, even a mule? Please?" The stable-keeper shook his head again, lank grey hair flying everywhere. "No, Sir Knight, we've not got anything at all. Well...no. No, nothing." The knight's eyes lit up. "You had an idea! What? Whatever it is, I'll take it and pay well." The stable-keeper sighed and said, "Well, it's not pretty, but we do have a specially-trained shaggy war-mastiff." "A war-mastiff?" asked the knight, "A dog? Show me!" So the stable-keeper escorted the knight into one of the stables. Inside was a dog like none the knight had ever seen. It was a giant, as tall at the knight himself. It also stank. It was the dirtiest, hairiest, mangiest, sorriest-looking dog that the knight had clapped eyes on in his entire life. He was revolted, but duty called..."It'll do," said the knight with resignation, "Saddle it up, stout stable-keeper." The stable-keeper nodded and headed over to the wall, where a saddle was hanging. As he reached for it, however, he started coughing so hard he convulsed. He fell on to the floor and lay there for 30 seconds, gasping, while the knight looked on impatiently. He recovered, got to his feet again, and reached for the saddle. Again, he was seized by coughing and convulsions, and he fell over. Finally, he struggled to his feet, looked and the knight regretfully, and said "I'm most dreadful sorry, sir knight, but I can't do it." "What?" asked the knight, thunderstruck, "Why not?" The stable-keeper shook his head. "I can't do it. I can't send a knight out on a dog like this."

✳✳✳✳

The Russians had been purchasing huge quantities of grain from the NATO countries. This placed Russia in a weak, dependent position so they instigated a research program and invested heavily. After a year or so Russian scientists discovered a new type of grain, called Krilk, that was good to eat, yielded twice as much as normal wheat and ripened in just half the time. The only catch was that it required special treatment during milling in order to provide usable flour. Well, that was OK, and huge prairies of Krilk sprung up all over Russia, along with super-secret milling stations, highly protected black buildings that took Krilk in one side and churned bags of flour out the other. The CIA teamed up with MI6 to discover the secrets of Krilk, either to appropriate it for the West or to find a way to stop production, because Russia was no longer dependent on the NATO countries. Either way, the key was the milling process. Teams of highly-trained infiltrators tried to get into the Krilk mills, but they all failed. Gorgeous femmes fatales attempted to seduce Krilk millers, but got nowhere; the pretty-boy gigolos did no better. Spy satellites could see the outside of the buildings, but not the milling process. Nothing worked. Someone even suggested offering to purchase the information through normal channels, but that suggestion was quickly squashed. One morning the Russian representative at the United Nations sent an offensive little note to the American and British representatives about the matter, which read, "Stop wasting your money and our time. The new super-grain will remain Russian secret. There is no use spying over milled Krilk."

Cole's Law – Thinly-sliced cabbage.

****

Deep in the jungles of Africa lived two tribes, and they hated each other. One tribe lived at the foot of a gigantic mountain. They panned for gold in the river and mined for gold in the mountain. There was lots of gold in the area, and they were extremely rich. The other tribe lived in a swampland area and lived on crocodiles and fish, and they had nothing. They were extremely poor. The tribes never visited each other except to raid each others' grass huts and plunder them. There wasn't much gain for the rich tribe in raiding the poor tribe, but they did it out of a sense of vengeance for the poor tribe's raids, and to try to get their stuff back. One day the Chief of the rich tribe got wind of a raid planned for the following day. The poor tribe were going to sneak in and steal his golden throne. The Chief was furious. Determined not to let them get away with it, he called his wise man over to advise him. The wise man told him, "Chief, you will have to make your throne disappear. Get some men to stick long wooden poles into the grass roof. Then, using ropes, your strongest men can hide the throne up in the roof of your grass palace. The raiders will never think to look up there." The Chief thought this was a great idea, and immediately ordered it to be done. The next day, as expected, the poor tribe attacked and swept through the village, searching everywhere. They didn't find a thing. The rich tribe were hiding in the mines in the mountains, and all the valuables were safely hidden away on top of the throne. When the raiders had gone the tribe came out and went back down to their village, and had a great celebration. The Chief stood in the centre of his palace, looked up at the roof, and gloated, "We fooled those idiots! Right over their heads, and they missed it!" Suddenly there were several tremendous bangs. The wooden poles supporting the gold throne snapped. Two tons of gold came crashing down on top of the Chief, and killed him stone dead — which just goes to show you that people who live in grass houses shouldn't stow thrones.

****

There was once a wise, sensitive guy (no, really!) who loved a beautiful girl. She lived in the middle of nowhere, in a marsh where his car always got stuck. To make matters worse, her father had a gun and disliked the guy. Although the girl was fond of him, he could only get to see her by fooling her father into thinking he was someone else. However, he had a rival — a more energetic suitor. This second guy wasn't as wise or sensitive, but he was more persistent, so he bought a set of amphibious tyres for his car and, one night when her father was asleep, drove up and sneaked away with her. The moral of this is, of course, that treads rush in where wise men fear to fool.

****

How many existentialists does it take to change a light bulb? Two. One to screw it in, and one to observe how the light bulb itself symbolises a single incandescent beacon of subjective reality in a netherworld of endless absurdity, reaching towards the ultimate horror of a maudlin cosmos of bleak, hostile nothingness.

A crushingly poor farmer was down to his last meal. The only thing he had in the world, apart from his mud hut and the rags he wore, was his talking mule. This particular talking mule had a snappy line in comedy, and a great stand-up routine with a dry, understated type of humour, so the farmer was reluctant to sell up, but there was no choice. With much regret, he set off to the city to sell the mule. Relying on the mule's natural talents, he stopped at a street corner and let the mule go for it. Well, the mule was so funny that within five minutes he had a whole crowd around, rolling in the street with laughter. One guy near the front said, "Look, I'm a talent agent, and I've got to have that mule." "What will you offer?" asked the farmer. "I don't have any cash," said the man, "but I'll tell you what. Here is my key-ring, my Porsche, my flat in town, my house in the country — they're all yours. These people here can bear witness to the deal." "Alright," said the farmer, and they made the exchange. The agent walked off with the mule, and most of the people followed, while the farmer adjusted to the idea of being a wealthy property-owner. "That didn't take long," he mused. "Ahh," replied a guy who hadn't left the area, "A mule that is funny is soon bartered..."

****

A team of scientists were nominated for the Nobel Prize. They had used dental equipment to discover and measure the smallest particles yet known to man. They became known as "The Graders of the Flossed Quark..."

****

An old farmer had spent his life collecting tractors. Whenever one finally broke down or became hopelessly out of date, he refused to sell it, instead keeping it in a large barn. He even bought tractors that were no longer any use from other farmers. He tidied up the bodywork and polished them, treating them like museum exhibits. Eventually, when it was time for him to retire, he decided to sell off his massive collection so that he could live comfortably with his wife in a nice country cottage. So he put advertisements in local and national papers, inviting offers. He didn't have long to wait. A few days later, he received a letter from a businessman whose company had built some of the tractors mentioned in the advert many years before, and who had an interest in old vehicles himself. The two men arranged to meet in the farmer's local pub on the following Sunday. The day came and the businessman arrived. Despite the heavy clouds of pipe smoke, the two passed an hour in most pleasant conversation, and turned out to have much in common. "Well," sighed the farmer eventually, "I haven't had such a good natter for a long time, but I suppose it's about time we got down to business, eh?" "Yes, I suppose so," replied the other, "but maybe we could go somewhere else? I'm finding it hard to think in such a smoky atmosphere." The farmer grinned, and said "Ah, there's no need for that. Watch this!" He then proceeded to take an amazingly long, deep breath, and sucked in every last wisp of smoke in the room. He then turned to the window behind him and blew all the smoke out of the pub. "Wow! How the hell did you manage that?" asked the businessman, astonished. "Oh, it was nothing," replied the farmer, "After all, I am an ex-tractor fan."

****

Would a pun about a Mexican long-haired chihuahua puppy qualify as a short shaggy dog story?

****

A group of whales were fed up with ships. The things criss-crossed their feeding grounds, migration paths and breeding areas all the time. Occasionally, they turned out to be actively hunting them. So, they held a strategic meeting in the middle of the ocean, and decided to hammer out a plan of action. "We'll split into two groups, one behind the other," said the chief whale. "The first group can swim under each ship, and everyone will blow together. This will create a huge bubble of air, which will capsize the ship, dropping the sailors into the water. The second group of whales, which will have to be you killer whales over there, can then eat them all up. Soon word will spread, and we'll be left alone." After the cheering died down, one whale towards the outside of the group raised a flipper to get some attention. The chief said, "Yes, Moby? You have something to add?" "Well," replied Moby, "I can go along with the blow-job, but I refuse to swallow any seamen."

****

A truck carrying copies of Roget's Thesaurus overturned on the highway. The local newspaper reported that onlookers were "stunned, overwhelmed, astonished, bewildered and dumbfounded."

****

A rich bloke decided to have himself cloned. After a long and expensive developmental process a clone was created and specially matured. Unsurprisingly, it turned out to be an exact physical duplicate of the man. Mentally, however, something went wrong, and all the clone could do was spew forth the most vile language and filthy profanities. After a couple of weeks of putting up with this torrent and trying to find out if the clone could respond or be somehow healed or repaired, the bloke decided to cut his losses. He took the clone up into the mountains, went to the edge of a steep cliff and pushed the clone over the edge. A policeman popped out from behind a tree and said, "I'm afraid you're under arrest, sir. I'm going to have to ask you to come with me." The bloke sighed, "Look, officer, it isn't what it looks like. I didn't murder anyone; that wasn't a real person." The officer shook his head. "I didn't say anything about murder, sir. I'm arresting you under suspicion of making an obscene clone fall."

A young guy had a job bagging groceries at the supermarket. One day, the shop got a flashy new machine for squeezing the juice out of fresh fruit. Because of the potential danger, someone from the shop would have to work the machine. Intrigued, the guy asked if he could switch jobs, but his request was denied. The store manager shook his head sadly, and said, "Sorry lad, but baggers can't be juicers."

****

One day a snail got fed up with his reputation for being slow. He decided that he should get himself a fast car to compensate. After checking out the markets, he decided to go for the new Japanese Nissda 950-Z, which was clearly the best buy on the market, doing 0-60 in just 4.3 seconds. He went down to a car showroom, and asked about availability. The dealer was only to happy to help, after seeing the snail's platinum credit card, and assured him that he could have the car ready the following day. "Okay," said the snail, "it's a deal. But can you rebadge it for me as a 950-S? Change the paint-work to include an S, and modify the badge at the back." "Well, I guess so," said the salesman, "but it'll cost extra. Why do you want it done?" The snail smiled, "I don't mind about the price. 'S' stands for 'snail'. It's really important to me that everybody who sees me roaring past knows who's driving." The salesman thought "Fair enough", and the deal was concluded. The snail picked his car up the next day, and could be found blasting down roads and motorways happily for the rest of his life. Whenever he shot past, the people saw him zoom by and said, "Wow! Look at that S-car go!"

****

So this bloke walks up to a Buddhist hot dog vendor and says, "Make me one with everything..."

****

A good fairy was flying along over the Great Plains in Africa one afternoon when she heard a soft crying below her. She landed to investigate and saw a little yellow frog sobbing his eyes out. Feeling sorry for him, the fairy asked why he was crying. "None of the other frogs will let me join in all their frog games, because I'm not green," he cried. "Don't be sad," replied the fairy, and with a wave of her magic wand, turned the frog green. Delighted, the frog admired himself and was surprised to find that his penis was still yellow. He asked the fairy about it and, embarrassed, she said, "I'm sorry, but there are some things that a fairy just can't do. If you find the wizard, he can fix things up for you." The little green frog croaked his happy thanks and hopped off to see the wizard. Feeling like a good Samaritan, the fairy took to the skies again and hadn't gone much further when she heard more crying, although this time it was booming and loud. Down she flew again, only to discover a pink rhino. Although she had a fairly shrewd idea of the answer, the fairy asked him why he was crying. "None of the other rhinos will let me join in all their rhino games, because I'm not grey." So, again she waved her magic wand, and turned the rhino all grey. Happy again, the rhino was examining himself when he noticed that his penis was still pink. He asked the fairy about it and, embarrassed, she said: "I'm sorry, but there are some things that a fairy just can't do. If you find the wizard, he can fix things up for you." The rhino, however, heard this news and burst into tears again. "I don't know how to find him!" he lamented. "Oh," said the fairy pointing back across the plain a short distance, "that's simple. If you're off to see the wizard, you want to follow the yellow-pricked toad."

This reporter was interviewing a wizened, decrepit, wrinkly old man about longevity. "Do you recommend any special diet for a long life?" she asked him. "Absolutely," said the man, "I drink six pints of beer and a bottle of whisky every day, and I smoke at least 60 cigarettes. My favourite food, which I eat at least four times a week, is chips cooked in lard, served with liver gravy, with a deep-fried, battered king-size chocolate bar for pudding." The reporter was astonished "Amazing!" she gushed. "How old did you say you were?" The old man nodded sagely, and said "28."

****

What do you call 20 floppy-eared mammals hopping backwards in a row? A receding hare line...

Lads'

Night Out

4

Jokes about Women

How do you describe the perfect blonde? She'd be three feet tall, with no teeth and a flat head to rest your pint on.

✱✱✱✱

How can you tell if an office has a blonde worker? There's a bed in the stockroom and big grins on all the bosses' faces.

✱✱✱✱

What's the similarity between an blonde girl and a dog's turd? The older they get, the easier they are to pick up!

✱✱✱✱

How many blonde girls does it take to make a chocolate chip cookie? Five. One to stir the mixture and four to peel the smarties.

✱✱✱✱

What do you call a blonde mother-in-law? An air bag.

✱✱✱✱

Did you hear about the blonde who thought an innuendo was an Italian suppository?

****

How does a blonde get pregnant? Christ, I thought blondes were dumb!

****

What nickname do blondes use to boost their popularity? "B.J."

****

What do blonde virgins eat? They're still on baby food, obviously.

****

You have to bury blondes in a Y-shaped coffin, because as soon as they're on their backs, their legs open.

****

Why do blondes wear green lipstick? Well, red means stop...

****

Why do blondes drive BMWs? Because they can spell the name.

****

How did the blonde burn her face? Bobbing for chips.

★★★★

What is the worst thing about having sex with a blonde? Those bucket seats are damned uncomfortable.

★★★★

How do you plant dope? You can start by burying a blonde.

★★★★

How can you tell if a blonde owns a vibrator? By the chipped teeth.

★★★★

How can you tell if a blonde has been in your refrigerator? Lipstick on your cucumbers.

★★★★

How do you get a blonde to get up off her knees? Cum in her mouth.

★★★★

Why do blondes have little holes all over their faces? They're from eating with forks.

****

How do you brainwash a blonde? Give her a douche and shake her upside down.

****

What two things up in the air will get a blonde pregnant? Her legs.

****

What happens when a blonde gets Alzheimer's disease? Her IQ increases.

****

What's the difference between a blonde and an ironing board? It's a real bitch trying to get the legs open on an ironing board.

****

Why do blondes drive cars with sunroofs? They've got more leg room.

****

What's the difference between a blonde and a limousine? There are people who haven't been inside a limo.

****

How many blondes does it take to play hide-and-seek? Oh, just one.

****

What's the difference between a blonde and a broom closet? You can only get two guys into a broom closet at the same time.

****

Why couldn't the blonde write the number 11? She didn't know which '1' came first.

****

How can you tell if a blonde writes mysteries? She has a chequebook.

Why did the blonde climb up onto the pub roof? She heard that the drinks were on the house.

****

How does a blonde turn on the light after sex? She opens the car door.

****

How do you know a blonde likes you? She fucks you two nights in a row.

****

Why do blondes insist on their partners wearing condoms? So she's got a doggie bag for later.

****

Why do blondes take the pill? So they know what day of the week it is.

****

How do you measure a blonde's intelligence? Stick a pressure gauge in her ear.

****

How do you tell if a blonde created your garden? The bushes are darker than the rest...

****

Why did the blonde die while drinking milk? The cow fell on her.

****

What is the difference between a blonde and the Grand Old Duke of York? The Grand Old Duke of York only had 10,000 men.

****

Why don't blondes double-up recipes at dinner parties? The oven doesn't go to 700 degrees.

****

Why do blondes have more fun? They're easier to amuse.

****

Why don't blondes work as lift attendants? They can't remember the route.

****

Why do blondes like lightning? They just love having their picture taken.

****

Have you heard that NASA recently hired a whole bunch of blondes? They're doing research on black holes.

****

Why do blondes wear earmuffs? To cut down the draught.

****

How many blondes does it take to make a circuit? Just two - one to stand in the bath tub, and one to pass her the hair dryer.

****

What does a blonde say after multiple orgasms? "Way to go, team!"

****

What's the difference between a blonde and a brick? After you've laid a brick, it doesn't follow you around whining for two weeks.

****

Why do brunettes take the pill? Wishful thinking.

****

How do you keep a blonde busy? Write "Please turn over" on both sides of a piece of paper.

****

Why is a blonde like a postage stamp? You just lick them, stick them, then send them off.

****

What's the difference between a blonde and a trampoline? You take off your shoes before using a trampoline.

What did the blonde say when she knocked over the priceless Ming vase? "It's OK, Daddy, I'm not hurt."

****

What do you call a woman who knows where her husband is all the time? A widow.

****

What do you get when you cross a blonde and a lawyer? I don't know. There are some things even a blonde won't do.

****

How does a blonde part her hair? By doing the splits.

****

A big-boobed waitress came up to a blonde in the café and asked her for an order. The blonde read her nametag, then said, "'Debbie.' Oh, that's sweet. What do you call the other one?"

A bloke received a telegram telling him that his mother-in-law had died and enquiring whether she should be buried or cremated. He replied immediately, saying, "Don't take any chances. Burn the body, then bury the ashes."

****

A blonde was standing on a street corner when a man stopped and said, "Excuse me, but do you know that you have a tampon hanging out of your mouth?" She went pale, and said, "Oh, my God! What did I do with my cigarette?"

****

A mother-in-law paid a visit to her daughter's husband. He opened the door and said, "Good afternoon, dear! I'm so glad to see you! It's been ages. Come in, please! How long are you staying?" The mother-in-law smiled and said, "Oh, until you get tired of me." The bloke looked at her and said, "Won't you at least have a cuppa?"

****

This woman was so jealous that when her husband came home one night and she couldn't find any unfamiliar hair on his jacket, she screamed at him, "God! Only you would cheat on me with a bald woman!"

****

What do you say to a blonde that won't have sex with you? "Have another beer."

****

A pair of newlyweds were on their honeymoon. The first night the groom asked, "Honey, you can tell me. Am I the first man?" She looked up at him and said, "Why does everybody always ask me that?"

****

This bloke was down the pub, chatting to his mates. "I called the local insane asylum this morning," he said, "to check on whether any inmates have escaped recently." One friend asks, "Oh? Why, feeling nervous?" "No," the bloke replied, "Somebody ran off with my wife last night!"

****

A bloke was travelling down a country road when he saw a large group of people outside a house. He stopped and asked a farmer why such a large crowd was gathered. The farmer replied, "Joe's mule kicked his mother-in-law and she died." "I'm impressed," replied the man, "she must have had a lot of friends." "Nope," said the farmer, "We're all here to bid for the mule."

****

A dentist told his female patient she needed a root canal operation. "I'd rather have a baby," replied the woman in disgust. The dentist said, "Well, you'd better make your mind up before I finish adjusting this chair."

****

"My husband is an angel," a woman said to her friend. "You're lucky," replied the friend. "Mine is still alive."

****

What do you say to a blonde with no arms and no legs? "Nice tits, love."

****

A wife was having coffee with a friend when she confided to her, "Our marriage has never been great, but this year has been an absolute nightmare. Bill shouts at me all the time, criticises me, puts me down, tells me I'm shit, never does anything at all around the house, and I know he's fucking that little tart of a secretary of his - I found her knickers in his briefcase. I can't eat, I can't sleep...in fact, I've lost eight pounds so far this month." "You should dump the bastard," her friend said, "then take him for everything he's got." The wife replied, "Oh, I'm going to, don't worry. First, though, I want to get down to eight stone."

****

A hippie with no job kept begging his girlfriend to marry him. She declined for months, saying he needed to get a job first. He always told her, "We can live on love, baby." Finally she relented, and they got married. The morning after their honeymoon, she got up, turned the cooker on to a low setting, and sat on the ring. "What are you doing, baby?" asked the hippie. "I'm heating your breakfast," she replied.

****

A woman asked her friend, "Would it kill you if your husband ran off with another woman?" The friend thought about it a bit, then said, "Well, it might. They say that sudden, intense delight can cause heart attacks."

What is the definition of gross ignorance? 144 blondes.

****

What's a 72? It's a 69 with three people watching.

****

What's five miles long and has an IQ of 40? A blonde parade.

****

It was this Essex bloke's first morning as a married man, and he'd had a wild night of mad sex with his new wife. Absent-mindedly forgetting where he was, he got up silently, dressed quickly, left fifty quid on the dresser and headed for the door. On the way out, he realised his mistake and sheepishly went back into the honeymoon suite. His new wife was there, tucking the cash into her bra...

****

What is the definition of the perfect woman? A gorgeous, deaf-and-dumb, blonde nymphomaniac whose father owns a pub.

What do you get by crossing a prostitute with an elephant? A whore who'll fuck you for peanuts and won't forget you afterwards.

****

What do you call a good-looking man with a brunette? A hostage.

****

Do you know what it means to come home to a man who'll give you a little love, a little affection and a little tenderness? It means you're in the wrong house.

****

What do you call a blonde sandwiched between two brunettes? A mental block.

****

What do you call a brunette with large breasts? A mutant.

****

What do you call a fly buzzing inside a blonde's head? A Space Invader.

****

What's the difference between a woman and a volcano? A volcano doesn't fake eruptions.

****

What do you call a basement full of women? A whine cellar.

****

What is the difference between a ten-year-old marriage and a ten-year-old job? After ten years, the job still sucks.

****

What was the blonde psychic's greatest trick? An in-the-body experience!

****

What do you call a brunette with a blonde on either side? An interpreter.

****

Bill and Kathy have gone to see their local vicar for some marriage counselling. After talking to them for a while, the vicar gets up and hugs Kathy, then sits down. He then gets up again and hugs Kathy a second and third time, before turning to Bill and saying, "Did you see that, Bill? Kathy needs that every single day!" Bill replies, "Well, I guess that's all well and good father, but I can only bring her over on Tuesdays and Thursdays."

****

What do you call it when a blonde dyes her hair brunette? Artificial intelligence.

****

A little boy at a wedding turns to his father and says, "Daddy, why is the girl wearing white?" His father replies, "The bride is in white to show that this is the happiest day of her life, son." The boy thinks about it, and then says, nervously, "Well then, why is the boy wearing black...?" His father nods slowly, and says, "You're catching on, son."

****

What's the difference between a dog scratching at the door and a woman scratching at the door? When you let the dog in, he'll stop whining.

****

Why do blondes wash their hair in the sink? Where else do you wash vegetables?

****

Why is a blonde like a door knob? Everybody gets a turn.

****

A blonde finally finished a jigsaw puzzle after six months, and she was really excited. On the box, it said, "From 2-4 years".

****

Why was the blonde upset when she received her driving licence? Because he'd given her an 'F' in sex.

****

I used to take my wife all over the place, but I've stopped now. There just wasn't any point. She always found her way back.

Why do brunettes sleep all night on their stomachs? Because they can.

****

Why don't women fart as much as men? Because they can't shut their mouths long enough to build up the pressure.

****

Why was the first football pitch sketched out on a brunette's chest? They needed a level playing field.

****

How are blondes like cornflakes? Because they're simple, easy and they taste good.

****

What's the difference between the Loch Ness Monster and a good woman? The Loch Ness Monster has, on occasion, been seen.

****

What has 80 balls and likes to screw little old ladies? Bingo.

****

How do you change a blonde's mind? Blow in her ear.

****

A bloke turned to his wife and suggested, "Let's go out and have some fun tonight." "Okay," replied the wife enthusiastically, "but if you get home before I do, leave the hallway light on."

****

How does a woman hold her liquor? By the ears.

****

What do you call a woman who can suck an orange through a hose pipe? "Darling."

****

69 + 69 = Dinner for four.

****

A bloke was at the altar getting married. The priest asked him to take his vows, and then he said, "I do." Immediately, his wife-to-be snapped, "Oh, no, you don't! I do!"

****

My wife is really immature. It's pathetic. Every time I take a bath, she comes in and sinks all my little boats.

****

In which month do women talk the least? February, of course. It's the shortest.

****

Why did the blonde cross the road? Road? What was she doing out of the bedroom?

****

The groom lay in bed on the first night of their honeymoon, while his blonde wife stood at the bedroom window, gazing at the stars. "Come to bed, darling," he whispered seductively after some time had passed. "Not likely," replied the bride, "my mother told me that this would be the best night of my life, and I'm not going to miss a minute of it."

****

What do you call a blonde with half a brain? Gifted!

****

A husband asked his wife, "Has the postman come yet, dear?" "No," she replied, "but he's panting hard and sweating a lot."

****

Phil came home from work and found his wife crying. "Your mother really offended me today," she sobbed. "My mother?" he asked. "How? She's on holiday in Australia!" "I know," she wailed. "This morning a letter addressed to you arrived, and I opened it, because I was curious." "Hmm, OK, and?" "Well, it was from her. At the bottom, she'd written 'PS: Dear Catherine, when you've read this, don't forget to pass it on to Phil.'"

****

An old man of 70 married a young girl of 18. When they went to bed the night after the wedding, he held up three fingers. "Oh, baby," said the young woman, "Does that mean we're going to do it three times?" "Nope," replied her husband, "it means you can take your pick."

****

How can you spot a woman wearing tights? Her ankles swell when she farts.

****

If a blonde is going to New York on a plane, how can you steal her window seat? Tell her the seats that are going to New York are the ones in the middle row.

****

Brian was dying, and his family were standing around the bed. In a weak voice, he said to his wife, "Dear, when I'm dead, I want you to marry Pete White." His wife was shocked, and said, "What? No! I couldn't marry anyone after you, darling." "But I want you to," said Brian. "Why?" asked his wife. "Well," he wheezed, "I've hated that bastard for 30 years."

****

What do a brunette and a freezer have in common? They've both got ice on the inside.

****

"If I died," asked Mike, "would you remarry?" His wife thought about it. "Well, I suppose so." "And would you and he sleep in our bed?" His wife thought again, and said, "I guess so. It makes sense." Mike pressed on, "Would you make love to him?" "Of course," replied his wife, "as he would be my husband then." "How about my golf clubs?" asked Mike, "Would you give those to him?" His wife shook her head. "There wouldn't be any point - he's left-handed."

How can two brunettes become invisible in a crowd of three? When they're with a blonde.

What did the blonde mother say to her daughter on Saturday night? "If you're not in bed by 12, come home."

What's the difference between a blonde and a cockerel? In the morning, a cockerel says, "Cock-a-doodle-doo", while a blonde says, "Any-cock'll-do."

Where did Prince Charles spend his honeymoon? In-Diana.

****

There is no reason for any wife to have an inferiority complex. All she has to do is to spend a week sick in bed and leave her husband to manage the household and the kids.

****

What's the difference between a blonde and a telephone? It costs 10p to use a telephone.

****

Why do brunettes like their hair dark? Because it doesn't show the dirt.

****

Did you hear about the blonde who waited up all night to see where the sun went? It finally dawned on her.

****

Why are brunettes flat-chested? It makes it easier to read their T-shirts.

****

Why is a brunette so proud of her hair? It matches her moustache.

****

Did you hear about the new girlie mag that caters for the married market? It's just like Playboy or Penthouse, but it's all the same model, month after month after month...

****

What does a blonde say when you ask her whether her indicator is working or not? "Yes, it is. No, it isn't. Yes, it is. No. it isn't..."

****

What's the difference between a brunette and a jelly? A jelly wobbles when you eat it.

****

Ian and Polly had just got married and were driving to Blackpool for their honeymoon. Along the way Ian, who was at the wheel, reached over shyly and stroked Polly's knee. Polly smiled, and blushed, and said, "We're married now, love. You can go farther if you want." So they drove to Edinburgh instead.

****

An elderly woman hurried up the stairs to the church, late for the wedding. An usher politely asked to see her invitation. "I don't have one," she said. "Well then," he said, "are you a friend of the groom's?" "I should think not," snapped the woman. "I'm the bride's mother."

****

What's the difference between a Rottweiler and a brunette with PMS? Lipstick.

****

How can you tell when a brunette's been using a computer? There are lipsticks marks on the screen.

****

Which disease paralyses women from the waist down? Marriage.

****

Generally speaking, mothers-in-law are generally speaking.

****

What's the difference between northern girls and southern girls on a date? Southern girls say, "Alright, I'll go to bed with you." Northern girls say, "Alright, I'll go to bed with all of you."

****

What did the blonde's right leg say to her left leg? Nothing. They had never met.

****

What do performing cunnilingus and being in the Mafia have in common? One slip of the tongue and you're in shit.

****

What is most women's idea of a perfect man? A bloke who is two-and-a-half feet tall, has a ten-inch tongue, and can breathe through his ears.

Why did they stop producing brunette Barbie dolls? Parents were scared that the dandruff might be contagious.

****

What does marriage teach women? Patience.

****

A blonde ordered a pizza and the guy behind the counter asked if he should cut it into six or eight slices. "Oh, six, please," said the blonde, "I could never manage eight slices."

****

What do you call a blonde with two brain cells? Pregnant.

****

How do you drown a blonde? Glue a mirror at the bottom of a swimming pool.

****

For dinner, what does a blonde make best? Reservations.

****

What is it called when a brunette dyes her hair blonde? Self-improvement.

****

The following sign was seen in a small restaurant: "Thanks for visiting. If you liked the food, send your friends. If not, send your mother-in-law."

****

How can you tell if your wife is dead? The sex is the same, but the plates are stacked up in the sink.

****

How can you tell when a blonde has an orgasm? She drops her nail file.

****

How can you tell if a blonde is a good cook? She can get the pop-tarts out of the toaster in one piece.

****

A blonde heard that 90% of accidents occur around the home, so she moved.

****

The true sign of a tough woman is that she rolls her own tampons.

****

How do you make a blonde's eyes light up? Shine a torch into her ear.

****

Why do blondes have vaginas? So guys will talk to them at parties.

****

Why do female paratroopers wear jockstraps? So they don't whistle on the way down.

****

Why did God create brunettes? So ugly men would have someone too.

****

What do you call a brunette whose phone rings on Saturday night? Shocked.

****

What's the best way to describe a blonde surrounded by drooling idiots? Flattered.

****

How do you get a blonde to marry you? Tell her she's pregnant.

****

How do you make a blonde laugh on Monday morning? Tell her a joke on Friday night.

****

What do you call a brunette in a waterbed? The dead sea.

****

When you gaze into a blonde's eyes, what do you see? The back of her head.

****

The night before her wedding, a young woman had a talk with her mother. "Mum," she started, "I want you to teach me how to make my new husband happy." The mother took a deep breath, steeled herself, and began, "When two people admire, honour, and respect each other, love can be a very beautiful thing..." "I know how to fuck, mum," the young woman interrupted. "I want you to tell me how to make that wonderful lasagne you do."

****

What do women and rocks have in common? The flat ones get skipped.

****

What do brunettes miss most about a great party? The invitation.

****

The morning after throwing a party for his boss, Nigel was nursing a king-size hangover and, finding his memory a bit sketchy, asked his wife, "What the hell happened last night?" She shuddered. "As usual, you made a complete wanker of yourself in front of your boss," replied the wife. "Piss on him," answered Nigel husband. "You did," said his wife. "He fired you." Nigel grunted, "Well, fuck him then." "I did," she replied, "and he gave you your job back."

****

What part of Popeye never rusts? His prick. He regularly dips it in Olive Oyl.

****

On their wedding night, a devout young man entered the bridal suite and found his wife lying languorously on top of the covers, naked. "I expected to find you on your knees by the side of the bed," he said disapprovingly. "Well, if I must," she replied, "but sucking cock always gives me hiccups."

****

At the marriage guidance bureau, a woman was complaining, "What's-his-name here says I don't give him enough attention."

****

Why can't brunettes do the splits? Their legs are welded together from the knee up.

****

How can you tell when a fax has been sent by a blonde? There's a stamp on it.

****

Why is sex with your wife like a late-night grocery? The goods are unattractively packaged, there's very little variety and there's a high price to pay, but there's just nothing else available at 2am.

****

How can you tell if a blonde's been using your computer? There's Tipp-Ex on the screen.

****

What do women and spaghetti have in common? They both wriggle when you eat them.

****

Down in Cornwall, they say that customs have changed very little over the centuries. Many a man still sleeps with a battle-axe by his side.

****

What do a blonde and a bottle of beer have in common? Both are empty from the neck up.

****

The good thing about dwarf brunettes is that they're only half as ugly.

****

Why do blondes have TGIF on their shirts? It stands for "Tits Go In Front."

****

A man answered a knock on his front door to find an Encyclopaedia Britannica salesman standing there. "Sorry," he said to the salesman, "We don't need it. My wife always assures me she knows all about everything going on."

What's the difference between vultures and mothers-in-law? Vultures don't pick on you until you're dead.

****

What's the first thing a blonde does in the morning? She walks home.

****

A couple were sitting in the living room watching TV. The phone rang, so the husband picked it up. He listened for a moment, and then said, in a sarcastic tone of voice, "I have no idea. Why don't you call the weather centre?" and hung up. "What was that all about?" asked his wife. "Oh, I don't know," replied the husband. "Some idiot wanted to know if the coast was clear."

****

How do you get a one-armed blonde out of a tree? Wave to her.

****

An old man had died. The funeral was in progress, and the vicar was talking at some length about the good life of the dearly departed, what an honest man he had been, what a loving husband and kind father, and how his poor family would miss him. Finally, unable to cope any longer, the widow whispered to her elder son, "Just pop on up there a moment and have a look in the coffin, will you? I want to be sure he's talking about your father."

****

What three little words does a wife most want to hear? "I'll mend it."

****

A doctor rushed out of his study. "Quick, grab my bag, darling!" he said to his lovely young wife. "Why?" she asked, alarmed. ."What's the matter?" "Some bloke just called and said he can't live without me," he gasped, reaching for his hat. His wife sighed. "Um, wait up a moment, will you," she said, gently. "I think that call was for me."

****

You know that your divorce proceedings are getting bitter and malicious when your lawyer no longer seems like a bloodsucking leech.

****

If a blonde and a brunette are thrown down a cliff, who hits the bottom first? It's the brunette. The blonde has to stop to get directions.

****

In the box that said, "Enter your husband's average income," the blonde wrote, "Oh, about midnight."

****

An upstanding, moral young man married a respectable convent girl, a young woman who had been kept away from the depravity of modern society. After the reception, the happy couple were on the way to the airport to go off on honeymoon. As they passed through one of the less pleasant areas of the city, she asked, "Darling, what are those women doing milling around dressed like that?" Her husband shook his head. "They're whores. They sell their sexual favours to men, for fifty quid a time." The bride was shocked. "Fifty quid? Those bastard monks only used to give us a damned apple afterwards."

****

How do brunettes comb the tangles out their hair after a shower? With a rake.

****

What is the advantage of having a blonde passenger? You can park in the handicapped zone.

****

What's the difference between a blonde and a toothbrush? Well, you wouldn't let your best friend borrow your toothbrush.

****

How do you confuse a blonde? Oh, you don't. They're born that way.

****

How do you know when a blonde has been making chocolate chip cookies? You find Smartie coatings all over the kitchen floor.

****

What's the difference between a woman and a computer? You only have to punch information into a computer once.

****

Steve was down the pub, nursing a beer in the corner. "Steve, mate, what's wrong?" asked the landlord. Steve sighed bitterly. "I had a quarrel with my mother-in-law. She swore to me she wouldn't talk to me for a month." The landlord looked puzzled. "What's so bad about that?" "You don't understand," sighed Steve. "That was four weeks ago, and today is the last day."

****

Are brunettes sexually active? Nope, they just lie there.

****

A newly-married couple checked into a hotel, and while they were signing in told the attendant that they'd just got hitched. "Congratulations!" said the girl, looking at the bride. "You'll be wanting the Bridal, then." "Oh, no thanks," replied the wife. "I'll just hold his ears until he gets the hang of it."

****

"Before I married my wife," this bloke complained, "everything was wine, women, and song. Now that I'm her husband it's all coffee, mother, and nagging."

"It's for my mother-in-law," a mourner leading a long funeral procession explained to an interested bystander. Tightening his leash, he gestured down at his dog and said, "My Doberman here mauled her one night." "God," sympathised the chap, "That's terrible. But...um...is there any way you might lend me your dog for a day or two?" The mourner jerked his thumb over his shoulder at the procession and answered, "I'm afraid you'll have to join the queue."

****

The doctor looked at the worried wife and said, "I'm going to be frank. I'm afraid your husband is at death's door." The wife said, "Isn't there any way you can open it and push him through?"

****

A man came home one afternoon and discovered his wife busily trying to cover up the obvious signs of wild sex. "Was it my friend Steve?" he yelled, furiously. "No," she said. "Well, was it my friend Rael?" he then asked. "Look," she shouted back, irritated, "don't you think I have any friends of my own?"

****

"Simon," his wife said, nose buried in the paper, "it says here that the government is going to trim down the navy. They're going to destroy six superannuated battleships." Simon looked up and said, "I'm sorry to hear that, dear. You'll miss your mother."

****

"You're claiming that several men proposed marriage to you," asked the incredulous husband. "Yes, several," his wife replied. "God! I wish you'd married the first idiot who proposed," he lamented. "I did," she sneered, "but the others proposed anyway."

****

"Alright," said the wife, "I'll admit that I like spending money, but it's the only extravagance that I have."

****

A really arrogant bloke was shagging a really arrogant bird. "God, aren't I tight, baby?" she moaned. "Nope," he grunted, "just stretched."

****

A woman went into a hardware shop to buy an axe. "It's for my husband," she told the assistant. "Did he tell you what poundage he was after?" asked the guy. "Are you joking?" she said. "He doesn't even know I'm going to kill him!"

****

According to a recent report, the most common marriage proposal in use today is: "You're WHAT?"

****

Why do brunettes have to pay extra for breast implants? Because the plastic surgeon has to start from scratch.

****

The best way to stop the noise in your car is to let her drive.

****

This Essex guy called his local tax office, and asked if he could write off the cost of his daughter's wedding against his tax bill as "a total loss".

****

You know that the honeymoon is over when the husband takes his wife off the pedestal and puts her on a budget.

Why do men pay a psychiatrist to ask a lot of expensive questions that their wives ask for nothing?

✱✱✱✱

This day of the year always brings back a lot of sad memories. It was two years ago to the day that I lost my wife and children. I'll never forget that poker game.

✱✱✱✱

Most husbands don't like to hear their wives struggling through the housework, so they turn up the volume.

✱✱✱✱

Never try to guess your wife's size when buying her clothes. Just buy her anything marked "petite," and keep the receipt.

✱✱✱✱

The law prohibits a man from marrying his mother-in-law - a classic example of useless legislation.

✱✱✱✱

It is better to have loved and lost than to have had to live with that bitch for the rest of my life.

My ex-wife is an excellent laxative...If the sight of her doesn't make you crap yourself, she'll irritate the shit out of you in a couple of hours.

****

One For The Ladies

5

Jokes about Men

Men say that women wear make up and perfume because they are ugly and smell bad. Why don't men wear make up and perfume, then? They're ugly and smell bad too, but they can't tell...

****

What do women do with their assholes in the morning? Pack them a lunch and send them off to work.

****

How do men sort their clothes? Into two piles - "filthy," and "filthy but wearable."

****

What is the thinnest book in the world? "What Men Know About Women."

****

A sleazy guy asked a pretty lift attendant, "Don't all these stops and starts get you pretty worn out?" She shook her head, and replied, "It isn't the stopping and starting that gets on my nerves. It's the jerks."

Two women had met for coffee. One noticed that her friend seemed troubled, and asked, "Is something wrong? You look stressed." Her friend sighed. "Well, my boyfriend just lost all his money and life savings in a nasty stock market crash. He's totally bankrupt," she explained. "Oh, that's dreadful," the other girl sympathised. "You must feel really worried about him." "Yeah, I am," replied her friend, "I don't know what he's going to do without me."

What is a bloke's idea of a good a seven-course meal? A hot dog and a six-pack.

Before you marry, a man will lie awake all night thinking about something you said. After you marry, he will fall asleep before you finish saying it.

What do you have when you've got two little balls in your hand? A bloke's undivided attention.

Where do you have to go to find a man who is truly committed? A mental hospital.

****

What do most blokes consider safe sex to be? A padded headboard.

****

What do you call six nude blokes standing on each others' shoulders? A scrotum pole.

****

What's easier to build, a snowman or a snow woman? A snow woman is easier, because once you've made a snowman you have to scoop all the snow out of his head and use it to make his testicles.

****

What do you call an intelligent man in England? A tourist.

****

What do you give to the man who has everything? A woman who can explain how to work it.

****

Why are men's brains larger than dogs'? So they don't screw women's legs at cocktail parties.

****

Men are like chocolates. They never last long enough.

****

What's the difference between a new husband and a new dog? A year later, the dog is still pleased to see you.

****

Colonel Sanders was a typical man. The only three things he cared about were legs, breasts, and thighs.

****

Sadly, all men are created equal.

****

What's the definition of a bachelor pad? A flat where all the house plants are dead but there's something growing in the fridge.

****

What do a clitoris, an anniversary and a toilet have in common? Men always miss them.

****

What is a man's idea of foreplay? Half an hour of begging.

****

Most men think Mutual Orgasm is an insurance company.

****

Where is a women's asshole while she is having an orgasm? He's at home, looking after the kids.

****

Women would be better off if men treated them like cars. They'd get lovingly rubbed all Sunday morning, filled to the brim twice a week and a damn thorough servicing every six months or 50,000 miles, whichever comes first.

****

Why is a singles bar different from the circus? At the circus, the clowns don't talk to you.

****

What should you give a man who has everything? Penicillin.

****

Why did God create man? Because a vibrator won't mow the lawn.

****

Do you know why the tribes of Israel wandered in the desert for 40 years? Even then, men wouldn't stop to ask directions.

****

Why do only 10% of men make it to heaven? If they all went, it would be sheer hell!

****

Most men prefer looks to brains, but that's because most men see more clearly than they think.

****

Why do so many women fake orgasm? Because so many men fake foreplay.

****

Why don't men get haemorrhoids? Because they are all perfect assholes.

****

Men are so reluctant to become fathers because they're still too busy being children.

****

Why don't men show their true feelings very often? They simply don't have any.

****

Why do blokes give names to their penises? Well, they don't like the idea of having a stranger make 90% of their decisions.

****

Men can't get mad cow disease. They're all pigs.

****

A man is like a snowstorm. You don't know when he's coming, how many inches you'll get or how long it'll stay.

****

The only way to make a husband love you and nobody else is to become his secretary.

****

Why do blonde women have bruises around their navels? Blonde men are stupid too.

****

What is the difference between savings bonds and blokes? It takes a few years, but eventually bonds mature.

****

I really didn't want to marry him for his money, but I couldn't find any other way to get at it.

****

Boys will be boys, but men will be boys too, and they're better at it, because they've had more practice.

****

You see plenty of clever blokes with thick women, but you hardly ever see a clever woman with a thick bloke...

****

How do men exercise on the beach? They suck in their stomachs every time they see a bikini.

****

Women find it so hard to track down sensitive, caring, good-looking men for the simple fact that they already have boyfriends.

If a man appears sexy, caring and clever, give him a day or two. He'll soon be back to his usual self.

****

What do you do when your boyfriend walks out? Close the door!

****

At 35, a woman thinks about having children. At 35, a man thinks about dating children...

****

What do you call a woman without an asshole? Divorced.

****

What is the difference between blokes and ET? ET phoned home.

****

Men are like toilets. They're all either vacant, engaged or full of crap.

****

What has eight arms and an IQ of 60? Four blokes watching a football match.

****

How many men does it take to change a light bulb? Four - one to screw it in and three friends to brag about how he screwed it.

****

"Adam," said God, "Adam, I have some good news and some bad news, my lad. The good news is that I gave you a penis and a brain. The bad news is that I could only fit in enough blood to work one of the two at any one time."

****

How can you tell the difference between a present your husband buys for the hell of it, and a present he buys because he's feeling guilty? The guilty present is nicer.

****

A bloke's idea of planning for the future is to buy two crates of beer rather than one.

****

You tell if a guy is playing around when he sends you love notes that have been photocopied, and begin with the phrase, "To whom it may concern..."

****

How can you tell when it's puppy love for a bloke? He slobbers all over you.

****

If a bloke is better than you at something, he will tell you how important it is. If you are better than he is, he will claim it's nothing useful.

****

What's the difference between pink and purple? The woman's grip.

****

How can you tell if a bloke is aroused? He's breathing.

****

How do you know if a man is lying? Easy - his lips are moving.

****

What's the most stupid part of a man's body? The penis. It has a head without a brain, it hangs around with a nutcase and it lives just around the corner from an asshole.

****

What do you instantly know about a well-dressed man? His wife is good at choosing clothes.

****

This guy left the pub early, hoping to get home early enough not to get into trouble with his wife. When he got home, he discovered that his wife was in bed with his boss. Back at the pub later, he was telling the landlord the story. "That's dreadful," sympathised the landlord. "What did you do?" "Well," said the guy, "I crept back out again and got back here as fast as I could. They were just getting started, so I reckon I've got time for a couple of extra beers."

****

If blokes are so clever, how come you always see signs reading "Danger! Men Working"?

****

What's the greatest mystery about men? How can they continue getting older yet still manage to remain so immature?

****

What did God say after creating man? "Hmm. I can do better than that."

****

A priest and nun were on their way back home from a seminary when their car broke down. The garage didn't open until the morning, so they had to spend the night in the village's only B&B. It only had one room available, though. The priest said, "Holy Sister, I don't think the Lord would object, under the circumstances, if we spent the night sharing this one room. I'll sleep on the sofa, and you can have the bed." "Yes, I think that would be fine," agreed the nun. They prepared for bed, said some prayers, and then each one took up their agreed place and settled down to sleep. Ten minutes passed, and the nun said, "Father, I'm terribly cold." "Okay," said the priest, "I'll get you a blanket from the cupboard." Another ten minutes passed, and the nun said again, "Father, I'm still terribly cold." The priest said, "Don't worry Sister, I'll get up and fetch you another blanket." Well, another ten minutes passed, and the nun spoke up again. "Father, I'm still terribly cold. I don't think the Lord would mind if we acted as man and wife just for this one night." "I think you're right," said the priest. "Get up and get your own damn blankets."

****

A sure sign that a man is planning to be unfaithful is when he has a penis.

****

What do ceramic tiles and blokes have in common? If you lay them properly the first time, you can walk on them for life.

****

How can you tell that soap operas are fictional? In real life, blokes are only affectionate in bed.

****

Men are like animals. They're messy, insensitive and potentially violent, but occasionally they make great pets.

****

Men call women 'birds'. It must be because of all the worms women pick up.

****

When a man puts his best foot forward, it usually ends up in his mouth.

****

Why do men like masturbation? It's sex with the only person they love.

****

Men like love at first sight, because it saves them such a lot of time.

****

The top ten rejections used by men, and what they really mean, are:

10. I see you as a sister. (You're ugly.)
9. There's too big a difference in our ages. (You're ugly.)
8. I don't think about you in 'that' way. (You're ugly.)
7. My life is too complicated right now. (You're ugly.)
6. I've already got a girlfriend. (You're ugly.)

5. I don't go out with women from work. (You're ugly.)

4. It's not you, it's me. (You're ugly.)

3. I'm concentrating on my career. (You're ugly.)

2. I'm celibate. (You're ugly.)

1. Let's be friends. (You're hideous.)

****

Why is it dangerous to let a bloke's mind wander? It's too little to be allowed out on its own.

****

The bloke said, "Since I first laid eyes on you, I've wanted to make love to you in the worst way." "Well," she replied, "you've succeeded."

****

"Can you beat my total of 71 men?" asked Suzie. "Perhaps," replied Jane, "provided you supply the whips."

****

Why is screwing a man like watching a TV drama? Just when things get interesting, it's finished until next time.

****

What's a man's idea of helping with the housework? Lifting his legs so you can vacuum under him.

****

Why do gentlemen prefer blondes? Men always like company on their own intellectual level.

****

What do you do if your best friend runs off with your husband? Well, you miss her dreadfully...

****

What's the difference between a pub and a clit? Blokes have no trouble finding a pub.

****

What do blokes and atheists have in common? Neither believe in a second coming.

****

Why do men love computers? No matter what mood they are in, they can always get a floppy in.

I only wanted to have a child, not marry one...

A bloke's idea of a serious commitment is, "Oh, alright, I'll stay the night."

****

What is the difference between a man and giving birth? One is terribly painful, sometimes almost unbearable, while the other is just having a baby.

****

What is the difference between a bloke and a catfish? One is a bottom-feeding scum-sucker, and the other is a type of fish.

How many times ever, in total, is a bachelor's bed made? One - when it was in the factory.

****

How many men does it take to wallpaper a house? Only four, but you have to slice them thinly.

****

Why do bachelors like clever women? Opposites attract.

****

Men would find that their marriages lasted longer if they paid less attention to prenuptial agreements and more to postnuptial affection and sex.

****

How do blokes define a romantic evening? Shagging.

****

What's the best way for a single woman to get rid of cockroaches? Ask them for a commitment.

****

There was this guy who left his wife. She gave birth to twins, and he wouldn't believe her when she said that there was no one else.

****

What do you call a man who expects to have sex on the second date? Slow.

****

Do you know why men have holes in the end of their penises? It is to allow oxygen into their brains.

****

How do you save a man from drowning? Take your foot off his head.

****

It would be wonderful if there was a potion that could give an average bloke the physique of Sylvester Stallone, the brains of Steven Hawking and the humour of Jo Brand. Of course, it could be horrendous. One little slip and you might end up with a bloke who had Jo Brand's body, Sylvester Stallone's brain, and the charm of

Steven Hawking. Actually, thinking about it, who could tell?

****

My boyfriend said that his doctor needed a urine sample, some faeces and a semen specimen. I told him, "Just hand them your boxers."

****

Why are so many men uncircumcised? The doctors were afraid of giving the infant brain damage.

****

What makes a man chase women he has no intention of marrying? I don't know, but it's the same thing that makes dogs chase cars they have no intention of driving.

****

What is the difference between a sofa and a bloke watching telly? The sofa doesn't keep asking for beer.

****

Whenever a man tries to hide his baldness by combing hair across his head, the truth comes shining through.

****

What do men and women have in common? Neither trust men.

****

Why do men like sleeping with virgins? They can't stand criticism.

****

Did you hear that they are going to stop circumcising men? They discovered they were throwing away the best bit.

****

Why don't women blink during foreplay? They simply don't have time.

****

Boyfriends are like cockroaches. They hang around the kitchen and are very hard to get rid of.

****

Real women don't have hot flushes. They have power surges.

****

Bankers are excellent lovers, because they have an excellent knowledge of the penalties for early withdrawal.

****

Why do men like frozen microwave dinners so much? They love being able to satisfy urges in under five minutes.

****

Why don't men have mid-life crises? They're all stuck in childhood.

****

Why does it take one million sperms to fertilise one egg? They won't stop to ask for directions.

****

Husbands are like lawn mowers. They're hard to get started, emit foul smells and don't work half the time.

****

What is the one thing that all the men at a singles bar have in common? They're married.

****

What do electric train sets and breasts have in common? They're intended for children, but it's the husbands who end up playing with them.

****

A man was sitting beneath a tree, thinking about how good his wife had been to him and how fortunate he was to be married to her. He asked God, "Why did you make her so kind-hearted, Lord?" The Almighty responded, "So you could love her, my son." The man nodded. "Why did you make her so good-looking, Lord?" "So you could love her, my son," replied God. "Why did you make her such a good cook, Lord?" he persisted. "So you could love her, my son," came the answer. The man thought about it. Then he said, "I don't mean to seem ungrateful or anything Lord, but why did you have to make her so stupid?" God sighed. "So she could love you, my son."

Two men who hadn't seen each other in years met on the street. While they were talking and trying to catch up on all those intervening years, one asked the other if he had got married. "Nope," the other man replied. "I look like this because someone just tipped a cup of coffee over me."

****

Two old men are sitting on a park bench watching the young women go by. One turns to the other: "You know, Pete, I'm still sexually interested in women. In fact, I always get excited when I see pretty young things walking by in those skimpy little numbers that are so fashionable nowadays. The problem is at my age I'm just not seeing so well any more."

****

A couple in their sixties, both of whom have lost their partners to illness, decide to get married and move to Bournemouth. To make sure that everything runs as smoothly as possible, they decide to organise the various details in advance. "What are we going to do about our old houses?" June asks Harry. He thinks about it, and replies, "Well, we ought to both sell our homes, and then we can both pay half of the cost of our new home. How do you want to organise the grocery bills?" June shrugs, and says, "Neither of us eat much, so we might as well just split the bill on a monthly basis. It's probably worth doing the same with the electricity and gas bills, too." Harry cheerfully agrees, and then asks his fiancée what she wants to do about sex. June shrugs, and says, "Infrequently, I think." "Tell me," replies Harry, "Was that one word or two?"

****

An old man and his wife decided to divorce. At the hearing, the magistrate was perplexed. Looking from one to the other in confusion, she said, "Mrs Matthews, you're 93. Mr Matthews is 95. You've been married for 74 years. Now, at such a venerable age, you want to divorce. Why? I don't understand." The old man shook his head and said, "That woman and I have loathed each other for 65 years." No less confused, the magistrate asked, "Why didn't you divorce earlier, then?" "It was the children, you see," replied the old woman. "We didn't want to hurt them, so we decided to wait until the last one had died."

****

What do you do if your bank account stops working? Ditch him.

****

Did you hear about the stupid guy who put ice in his condom? He wanted to keep the swelling down.

****

Why do doctors slap babies' bums after they're born? To knock the dicks off the clever ones.

****

Why do spiders kill the males after mating? To stop the snoring before it starts.

****

What do you call a handcuffed man? Trustworthy.

****

How many men does it take to change a roll of toilet paper? God knows. It's never happened.

****

Women are indeed silly. They sleep with men who - if they were women - they wouldn't even have bothered to have lunch with.

Most women's idea of the perfect man is someone who is obedient, well-mannered, faithful, can empty the garbage and is great in bed. If only you could train dogs to screw in positions other than doggie-style, and bestiality was more socially accepted...

****

Before money was invented, what did women find attractive about men?

****

The only time a woman values a man's company is when he owns it.

****

Why is psychotherapy so much quicker for men than for women? When it's time to take a bloke back to his childhood, he's already there.

****

Three guys were out fishing when one caught a mermaid. She offers to grant each fisherman one wish, in exchange for her freedom. "Alright, double my IQ," said the first fisherman. "Done," said the mermaid, and the man - to his amazement - began to recite

Shakespeare. The second fisherman was so staggered that he forgot all about making his dick larger, and said to the mermaid, "Triple my IQ!" "Done," said the mermaid, and he started deducing solutions to mathematical problems that he had never even realised existed. The third fisherman was beside himself. "Quintuple my IQ!" he screamed. The mermaid looked at him and said, "Normally I wouldn't try to change someone's minds about a wish, but I'd really like you to reconsider." The bloke shook his head stubbornly. "No, I want my IQ increased five times. If you don't do it, I won't set you free." "Please," said the mermaid, "it will alter your entire view of the universe." No matter what the mermaid said, the third fisherman insisted. So the mermaid sighed and said, "Done." With that, the third guy became a woman.

****

What is the most important thing about female astronauts? When the crew gets lost in space, at least the woman will ask for directions.

****

The only time that a man thinks about a candlelight dinner is when the power goes off.

Why do men snore? When they fall asleep, their balls flop over their assholes and form an airlock.

****

The only way to hurt a man with your words is to hit him in the face with your dictionary.

****

Single women claim that all the good men are married, but married women complain that their husbands are appalling. This proves, for once and for all, that there is no such thing as a good man.

****

How do you tell if a man is happy? Who cares?

****

While shopping, women get excited and happy when they buy that perfect item. Men experience the same feelings when they find a good parking space.

They say that men only think about sex. That's not true. They're also fixated on power, world domination, money, football and beer.

****

Men are like adverts. You can't believe a word they say.

****

Why are blokes like UFOs? You don't know where they come from, you don't know what their mission is and you don't know what time they're going to take off.

****

When he asks you if he's your first, say, "I'm not sure. You might be. You do look slightly familiar."

****

Men are like blenders. You have this feeling that you need one, but you're really not sure why.

Why is a bloke like a diploma? You spend lots of time getting one, but once you have it, you don't really know what use it is.

****

If he asks you if you're faking it, tell him, "No. I'm just practising."

****

If you think he's listening to you, you're wrong. He's trying to find the childish innuendoes in what you just said.

****

"I don't know why you wear a bra," said the husband, "You've got nothing to put in it." "You wear boxers, don't you?" replied the wife coolly.

****

What's the difference between men and pigs? Pigs don't turn into men when they get drunk.

****

How do men define a '50/50' relationship? Women cook and they eat; women clean and they make messes; women iron clothes and they wrinkle them.

****

When a man says, "I hate to go shopping," he means "...because I always end up outside the changing room, holding your purse."

****

When a man says, "Can I help with dinner?" he means, "Why isn't it on the table?"

****

"Did you see that guy?" a woman asked a friend. "He doesn't sweat!" The second woman replied, "Yes, I know. Snakes generally don't."

****

When a man says, "Football is a man's game," he means, "Women are too sensible to play it."

When a man says, "Ask your mother," he means, "I am unable to make any decision."

****

When a man says, "Good idea," he means, "It'll never work, and I can spend the rest of the day gloating about it."

****

When a man says, "Have you lost weight?" he means, "I've just blown our last £50 on a power drill."

****

When a man says, "I've read all the classics," he means, "I collect Playboy, and have done since 1972."

****

When a man says, "I've got my reasons," he means, "I'll think of something soon."

When a man says, "Darling, we don't need material objects to prove our love," he means, "Fuck! I forgot our anniversary again!"

****

When a man says, "I split up with her," he means, "She ditched me."

****

When a man says, "I brought you a present," he means, "I won a free paperweight as a booby prize in the pub's meat raffle."

****

When a man says, "She's one of those rabid feminists," he means, "She refused to make me a cup of tea."

****

When a man says, "That's women's work," he means, "It's difficult, dirty and thankless."

When a man says, "Will you marry me?" he means, "Both my flatmates have moved out, I can't find the washing machine and the bin is full of pizza boxes."

****

When a man says, "You look terrific," he means, "Oh, please don't try on any more outfits. I'm starving."

****

The only problem with women is men.

****

Women prefer the simple things in life...like blokes.

****

Boy will be boys, but one day all girls will be women.

****

Every man has it in his power to make one woman happy...by remaining unmarried.

The trouble with some women is that they get all excited about nothing, and then marry him.

The average man is proof that women can take a joke.

They put a man on the moon. Why can't they put them all there?

If you catch a man, throw him back!

If men got pregnant, abortions would be carried out in high-street stores and at drive-throughs.

Only a man would buy a £300 car and put a £2,000 stereo in it.

****

Diamonds are a girl's best friend, while dogs are a man's best friend. You tell me which sex is smarter...

****

Men would rather pledge loyalty to a flag than to a woman.

****

Don't trust a man who says he's single and then collects you in a Volvo estate with a child seat in the back.

****

So many men, so many reasons not to shag any of them.

****

There are only two four-letter words that are offensive to men - "stop" and "don't".

****

Short skirts remind blokes of their manners. Have you ever seen a bloke push on to a bus in front of a girl in a short skirt?

****

Scientists have just discovered something that can do the work of five blokes - one woman.

****

Marrying a man for money is a terrible mistake. You'll have to earn every penny.

****

A bachelor is a man who has missed his opportunity to make a woman miserable.

****

The best way to get a bloke to do something is to suggest that he is far too old for it.

****

Men who say they can see through women are missing a lot.

****

Man was made at the end of the week's work. God was tired.

****

An unmarried man is an example of the failure of the 'Care in the Community' scheme.

****

My ex-boyfriend and I weren't compatible. I'm a Libra and he's an asshole.

****

Men...give them an inch, and they add it to their own.

****

90% of men give the other 10% a bad name.

****

My ex-boyfriend was a poor communicator. It's hard to drink beer and talk at the same time.

****

Few women admit their age, but fewer men act theirs.

****

Men piss like cheap cameras - they just point and shoot.

****

Never hit a man with glasses - hit him with a baseball bat.

****

Pre-menstrual tension is something that makes women act once a month like blokes do every day.

****

The bloke who said that all men are created equal never went to a nudist colony.

****

Being a woman is quite difficult, because it mainly consists of dealing with men.

Professional Misconduct

6

Jokes about Medicine, Law and Other Professions

A doctor began his examination of an elderly man by asking him what brought him to the hospital. The old man looked surprised, and said, "Why, it was an ambulance."

****

A bloke went to a private urologist and said, "Doctor, I have a problem. My penis is garishly red." The urologist replied, "Well, okay, let's have a look at the old fellow then. Hmm...yes, no problem. We'll have you sorted out in no time." He told the bloke to lie down, then fiddled about a bit with the bloke's prick, did one or two things and said, "Right. All done; that'll be £50." Sure enough, the bloke's penis was back to normal. Impressed, he paid up. A couple of weeks later, he was chatting to a friend of his who looked a bit shifty and said, "You know, I've got the same problem, but it's greenish, not red. That specialist sounds cheap – I'll go and try him out." So the next day the friend went to the same doctor. He showed the urologist his penis, and the chap said, "Hmm...well, we can sort you out, but it's going to cost you £4,100, I'm afraid, and we'll have to operate." The bloke looked at the doctor in horror. "£4,100 and an operation? You sorted my mate out for fifty quid!" "That's very true," nodded the doctor, "but he had lipstick smudges on his old chap. You've got gangrene!"

This Australian guy living in London went to see his GP. He walked in, and said, "Doc, it's my prick," then unzipped his fly and unfurled a thick, 12-inch penis, lovingly tattooed with a dragon, on to the doctor's desk. The doctor peered at it and asked, "And what appears to be the problem?" "Aw, there's no problem, doc," replied the Aussie. "He's a beaut, though, ain't he?"

****

Two psychiatrists walked passed each other in the corridor. "Morning," said one, and nodded. "I wonder what he meant by that,' worried the other.

****

This bloke has just finished his painless five-minute check-up at the dentist's. "It must be a real bugger spending all day with your hands in people's mouths," he said. The dentist grinned. "I think of it as spending all day with my hands in their wallets. That'll be £25, please."

****

A man telephoned the mental hospital and enquired as to who was in Room 23. "That room is empty," replied the nurse. "Great!" said the bloke, "That means I must have escaped!"

****

A proctologist pulled a thermometer out of his inside jacket pocket. He looked at it in horror and said, "Shit! Some arsehole has walked off with my pen!"

****

A bloke was the private patient of a doctor mate of his. He went to see his pal one afternoon, explained his problem, let the guy look him over and then took a prescription from him. "Ah, lovely. Thanks, Ed," he said. "Since we're such good friends, I'm not going to insult you by offering to pay, but I'd like you to know that I have made a provision for you in my will." The doctor nodded and, touched, said, "That's very kind. Uh, Paul, before you leave, could I just have that prescription a moment? There's one little thing I need to correct..."

****

Old dentists never die; they merely get a bit long in the tooth.

****

At a medical convention, a respected specialist gave a speech detailing a miraculous new antibiotic he had discovered. "What will it cure?" asked someone in the audience. "Oh, nothing that seven or eight other antibiotics won't fix more quickly," he replied. "What's so miraculous about that?" asked the questioner, surprised. "It has a major side-effect of short-term memory loss," explained the specialist. "Several of my patients have paid their bill three, four, even five times..."

What is 18 inches long and can be found hanging in front of an arsehole? A stethoscope.

****

A vet was feeling ill, and went to see her GP. The doctor asked her all the usual questions, such as which symptoms she had, how long they had been occurring, and so on, when she sneered and said, "I'm not very impressed. As a vet, I've been trained to find out what is wrong with my patients by direct observation. Why do you need to ask so many questions? Don't you know what you're doing?" The doctor nodded, and said, "That's a fair point." He looked her up and down, then wrote out a prescription. As he handed it to her, he said, "There you are. Of course, if it doesn't help, we'll have to have you put down..."

****

A new nurse spotted a couple of surgeons grubbing around in the flower-beds outside the front of the hospital. "Excuse me, doctors," she said, "Can I help at all? Have you lost anything?" "Oh, no, thank you, nurse," replied one. "We're prepping a heart transplant for a tax inspector, so we're just hunting for a suitable stone."

****

The worst thing you can hear as the anaesthetic starts to hit is, "Lord of This World, Father of Lies, Prince of Darkness, accept this, our Sacrifice..."

****

An elderly bloke goes to his doctor to get the results of some check-ups. He sits down, and notices that the doctor has a grave look on his face. "Some bad news, I'm afraid. The worst of it is that you have cancer, and only have six months to live." The elderly bloke is devastated. "Is there more, doctor?" "Yes, I'm afraid so," replies the doctor. "You have Alzheimer's." The elderly bloke's face lights up. "Thank God! I was sure I had cancer!"

****

A young woman went to the doctor and told him, "Doctor, I've got a problem. I'll need to undress to show you." The doctor nodded for her to continue, so she stood up, unzipped her dress and stepped out of it. "It's these," she said, pointing to the inside of her thighs, where two bright green circles were clearly visible. The doctor came round for a closer look, rubbed the circles and nodded thoughtfully. "Tell me," he asked, "do you have a gypsy lover?" The woman blushed, and said, "Well, um, yes, actually I do." "There you go then," said the doctor. "You'll have to tell him that his ear-rings aren't actually made of gold!"

****

I had to kill my psychiatrist. He helped me a lot, but he just knew too much.

****

This bloke dropped out of medical school. It was tragic. He really wanted to be a doctor, but he just couldn't stand the sight of cash.

****

"Would you do me a huge favour and scream in agony a few times?" asked the dentist pleadingly. "I'd really appreciate it." His patient looked dubious. "Well, OK," she said, "but would you mind telling me why first?" "Oh," he said, "The football's on in an hour, and I've got too many patients waiting to stand a chance of making it!"

****

"How much will it cost to have the tooth extracted?" asked the patient. "£50," replied the dentist. "£50 for a few moments' work?!" asked the patient. The dentist smiled, and replied, "If you want better value for money, I can extract it very, very slowly..."

****

An inmate went to see the prison doctor, and was dismayed to be told that he needed to have one of his kidneys removed. "Look," said the prisoner, "You're already whipped out my tonsils, my adenoids, my spleen and my gall-bladder, and now you want my kidney? I only came to you in the first place to see if you could get me out of here!" The doctor was unruffled. "And that's exactly what I am doing," he replied, "bit by bit..."

****

Mrs Jones got last-minute nerves about her plastic surgery operation. "Is it going to hurt, doctor?" she asked. "No, madam," he replied, "not until you get my bill."

"Doctor, my hair keeps falling out. What can you give me to keep it in?" "Will a shoebox do?"

****

A man walked into the psychiatrist's office with a bit of buttered toast on his head, fried eggs on each shoulder, a sausage in his left nostril and a strip of bacon tied to each eyebrow. The psychiatrist looked at him, then calmly asked, "What seems to be the problem, sir?" The man looked at him, and replied, "Well, I'm really worried about my brother."

****

If there's one thing worse than your doctor telling you that you have venereal disease, it's your dentist telling you...

****

Howie had been feeling guilty all day long. He kept trying to put it out of his mind, but he couldn't: the sense of betrayal was overwhelming him. Every so often his soothing inner voice would try to rally his defences, saying reassuringly, "Howie, don't worry. You aren't the first doctor to sleep with a patient, and certainly you won't be the last." Invariably, though, the sneering voice of guilt would interrupt, accusing, saying, "Howie Reed, how can you call yourself Basingstoke's top vet?"

****

If I have sex with my clone, will I go blind?

****

A doctor and his wife were having a big argument over breakfast. "Well, you're no bloody good in bed either!" he yelled, and stomped off to work. By midday, he had relented, and decided he'd better apologise. He called home, and after a great many rings, his wife picked up the phone. "What took you so long to answer?" he asked. "I was in bed," came the reply. "What were you doing in bed this late?" There was a moment's silence; then she said archly, "Getting a second opinion."

****

There was a young dentist called Sloan,
Who catered to women alone,
In a moment's depravity,
He filled the wrong cavity,
And said, "Look! My business has grown!"

A mute bloke was walking down the street when he passed a friend of his. He tapped him on the shoulder, and asked how things were, in sign language. "Oh, pretty good actually," replied his friend, vocally. "As you can hear, I can talk now." Excited, the bloke asked for details. "Well," said his friend, "I went to a specialist who found I had no physical damage, and he put me on a program of treatment that eventually gave me the power of speech. It's wonderful." At the bloke's insistence, the friend cheerfully gave him the doctor's phone number; then, realising his mistake, laughed and gave him the address. Well, the mute bloke went along that afternoon. As luck would have it, there was a spare appointment time, so the specialist examined him and found that he, too, could be treated. The mute indicated that cost was no object – he'd pay whatever it took – and said that he'd like to start as soon as possible. "Very well," replied the doctor, and told him to go into the treatment room, get undressed, and lean over the table that was there. While the mute bloke did so the doctor got a broom handle, a hammer and a jar of Vaseline. He thoroughly lubricated the broom handle, then crept into the other room, where the mute was waiting, arse in the air, positioned the handle by the bloke's arsehole, then whacked it deep up his bottom with a firm stroke of the hammer. "AAAAAAAAAAAAAA AAAAAAAAAAAAA!" screamed the mute in agonised horror. "Excellent!" congratulated the doctor. "Come back on Wednesday, and we'll get to work on 'B'..."

A doctor thoroughly examined his patient, and said, "Look, I really can't find any reason for this mysterious affliction. It's probably due to drinking." The patient sighed, and snapped, "In that case, I'll come back when you're damn well sober!"

****

You can always tell when a death certificate has been completed by a Russian doctor. He signs in the 'Cause of death' box...

****

A handsome doctor was so vain that whenever he took a woman's pulse he adjusted the results downwards by 10 over 2 to compensate for the fact that he had touched her.

****

Did you hear about the mystic who refused anaesthetic for his tooth extraction? He wanted to transcend dental medication.

****

"Tell me nurse, how is that boy doing; the one who ate all those 5p pieces?" "Still no change, doctor."

****

"Doctor, Doctor, I've got five penises," said the worried patient. "How do your trousers fit?" asked the doctor curiously. "No problem," the guy replied. "They fit like a glove."

****

American doctors have the letters "MD" after their names to warn you that they are Mentally Deficient!

****

"Did you take the patient's temperature, nurse?" "No, doctor. Is it missing?"

****

What is the difference between a genealogist and a gynaecologist? One looks up the family tree and the other looks up the family bush.

****

The doctor looked at his patient. "Tell me, does it hurt when you do this?" The patient winced, and said, "Yes, doctor." The doctor nodded sagely. "Don't do it, then."

****

When a car skidded on a wet road and struck a telegraph pole, several bystanders ran over to help the driver. A woman was the first to get to the victim, but a bloke rushed in and shouldered her out of the way. "Step aside, love," he said, "I've got a certificate in first aid." The woman observed for a minute or so, then tapped the bloke on the shoulder. "I just thought you should know that when you get to the part about calling for a doctor, I'm right here."

****

Did you hear about the nurse who swallowed a scalpel by mistake? She gave herself a tonsillectomy, an appendectomy and a hysterectomy, and circumcised three of the doctors.

****

A famous artist started to lose her eyesight at the height of her career. Understandably concerned, she went to the best eye surgeon in the world, and after two months of painstaking treatment and delicate, intricate surgery, her eyes were repaired. She was extremely grateful, so in addition to paying his bill, she painted him a gigantic water-colour of a vivid eye, and had it hung in his office one weekend. The press were fascinated, so she and the doctor held an unveiling of the new masterpiece, followed by a press conference. "Tell me, Doctor

Schwartz," said one journalist, "what were your first thoughts on seeing this exquisite new work of art?" The doctor shrugged, and replied, "I thought 'Thank Christ I'm not a gynaecologist!'"

****

"Doctor, should I file my nails?" "No, madam; throw them away like everybody else."

****

A man goes to the doctor and says, "Doctor, I've got this problem you see, only you've got to promise not to laugh." The doctor replies, "Of course I won't laugh, that would be thoroughly unprofessional. In over twenty years of being a doctor, I've never laughed at a patient." "OK then," says the man, and he drops his trousers. The doctor is greeted by the sight of the tiniest penis he has ever seen in his life. Unable to control himself, he falls about laughing on the floor. Ten minutes later he is able to struggle to his feet and wipe the tears from his eyes. "I'm so sorry," he says to the patient, "I don't know what came over me, I won't let it happen again. Now what seems to be the problem?" The man looks up at the doctor sadly and says, "It's swollen."

****

A man takes his dog to the vet, because the dog has been feeling poorly of late. In the surgery the vet examines the dog, taking temperature, feeling the dogs abdomen and smelling his breath. The vet steps back and shakes his head ruefully. "I'm sorry" he says, "Your dog has kidney failure. He has two days left to live." The man is appalled at this terrible diagnosis, and demands a second opinion. "Well, okay" says the vet, and picks up the phone. He mutters into the receiver for a few seconds and then puts the phone down. A minute later a cat comes into the surgery. The cat looks the dog over for a short while, and then turns to the vet and says "Kidney failure?" "That's what I thought" says the vet. "Yep. I'd say he has two days, maybe three," and the cat walks out. The man reacts angrily to this. "What the hell was that? I'm not taking a cat's opinion. Get someone else." The vet replies "Okay" and picks up the telephone again. After a short conversation, and a little wait, a Labrador walks into the surgery. The Labrador examines the other dog briefly and then announces, "Kidney failure, by the look of it. Not much more than two days left in the old boy." "I concur" says the vet and the Labrador leaves the room. The man has had enough and decides to go, "Right. I'm leaving." "That will be £450" says the vet. "What! That's a fortune! What the hell do you think you're playing at!" "Well, if it had just been me" says the vet "it wouldn't be that much, but after the cat scan and the lab report..."

****

A woman went to the doctor with bad knee pain. After the scans had been run without any obvious causes turning up, the doctor asked, "Can you think of anything you might be doing that could be causing this irritation to your knees?" The woman looked a bit sheepish, and said, "Well, Sid and I screw doggy-style on the floor every night." The doctor looked severe, and said, "That would do it, all right. You'll have to change that. There are plenty of other positions you could have sex in, you realise." "Not so that you can both see the telly," she shot back.

****

There was a bloke whose tongue was so long that when he stuck it out for the doctor, it was the nurse who said, "Ohhhhhhh!"

****

How can you tell the head nurse? She's the one with scuffed knees.

****

"Doctor, what fish did you say I had?" "You don't have a fish, you idiot! You've got cancer!"

****

A depressed bloke turned to his friend in the pub and said, "I woke up this morning and felt so bad that I tried to kill myself by taking 50 aspirin." "Oh, man, that's really bad," said his friend, "What happened?" The first man sighed, and said, "After the first two, I felt better."

****

"Doctor, what should I do if my temperature goes up by more than a point?" "Sell! Sell!"

****

This bloke went to the doctor and said, "My tongue tingles when I touch it to a hard-boiled egg wrapped in baking foil taken from the bottom of the toaster. What's wrong with me?" The doctor looked at him. "You have far too much spare time."

****

My father always thought laughter was the best medicine. That's probably why half of us died from tuberculosis.

****

Four nurses decided to play jokes on the doctor they worked for, because he was an arrogant tosser. That evening, they all got together on a break and discussed what they had done. The first nurse said, "I filled his stethoscope with cotton wool so he won't be able to hear anything." The second nurse said, "That's nothing! I drained the mercury out of his thermometers and painted them so that they all read 106 degrees." The third nurse said, "Well, I did worse than that. I stabbed tiny holes in all his condoms; you know, the ones he keeps in his desk drawer." The fourth nurse just fainted.

****

If you cloned Henry IV, would he be Henry V, or Henry IV Part II?

****

Alzheimer's Disease has lots of advantages. You get to hide your own Easter eggs and buy yourself surprise presents. You are always meeting new people. Best of all, you never have to watch repeats on television!

****

A patient with a sore throat goes to see his doctor. After examining him, the doctor says, "I'm afraid your tonsils will have to be removed." "I want a second opinion," says the man, unhappily. "OK," replies the doctor, "You're damn ugly, too."

****

An obese bloke visited his doctor, suffering from headaches. "Please get undressed," said the doctor, so the bloke did, puzzled. "Ah, excellent," said the doctor. "Now, please go and stand in the window, facing out, and thrust your penis towards the glass." Even more confused, the bloke obeyed. While he was standing there waving his flabby bollocks out of the window, he asked, "Look, doctor, I don't mean to criticise, but what has this got to do with my headaches?" The doctor was silent for a moment, then replied, "Nothing, actually. My ex-wife works in the office opposite my window."

****

"What kind of job do you do?" a woman asked the bloke next to her on the train. "Actually, I'm a naval surgeon," he replied. "Goodness!" said the woman, "You doctors do specialise in some arcane fields!"

****

A woman went to see her psychiatrist. "I'm really concerned," she said. "Yesterday, I found my daughter and the little boy next door together, naked, examining each other's bodies and giggling." The psychiatrist smiled. "There's nothing to worry about," she said, "It's not unusual." "Well, I don't know," said the woman, "It bothers me. It bothers my daughter's husband, too."

****

A woman visited her doctor for some advice. "Doctor," she asked nervously, "can anal sex make you pregnant?" "Of course," replied the doctor. "Where did you think we got lawyers from?"

****

A mother took her 17-year-old daughter to the gynaecologist and asked him to examine her. "She's been having some strange symptoms, and I'm worried," said the mother. The doctor carefully examined her daughter and then announced, "I'm afraid she's pregnant, madam." The mother gasped, and went pale. "What? That's impossible! My little darling has nothing to do with all those horrible men! Tell him, dear." "Yeth," lisped the girl fussily, "Thath abtholutely right. I've never even kithed a man!" The doctor looked at the mother, then at the daughter, then he got up and went over to the window and stared out. He stayed there for several minutes, until the mother finally asked, "Doctor, is there something wrong?" The doctor shook his head. "No, madam. It is simply that the last time anything like this happened, the father lit a star up out in the east, and I was just checking if another one had appeared."

****

A doctor lost his practitioner's license when he was caught having sex with one of his patients. It was a particular shame, as he had been the best mortician in town.

****

Scientists say that 92% of all ten-pound notes carry germs. That's not true. Not even a germ could live on a tenner.

****

What did the accordion player get on his IQ test? Spittle.

****

How can you tell when the stage is level? The drummer drools out of both sides of his mouth.

****

Why do some people have an instant hatred of jazz players? It saves time in the long run.

****

How can you tell the difference between heavy metal songs? By their names.

****

What is the definition of perfect pitch? Throwing a violin down a toilet without hitting the seat.

****

What's the difference between a banjo and a chainsaw? A chainsaw has a dynamic range.

****

How can you tell if there's a banjo player at your front door? He can't find the key, the knocking speeds up, and he doesn't know when to come in.

****

I recently had surgery on my hand. I asked the doctor if, after surgery, I would be able to play the accordion. He looked at me and replied, "I'm operating on your hand, not giving you a lobotomy."

****

A bloke decided to take a holiday and travel somewhere exotic, so he booked a trip to a small, relatively unspoiled Pacific island where the native culture was still intact. He flew into Thailand and set sail from Jakarta on a specially chartered boat to the island paradise. As the boat was approaching the island, he noticed the sound of drums. "How quaint," he thought, "the natives are performing an ancient drum ritual." He arrived at the island, and got something to eat in a charming local bar. He finished his meal, but the drums were still throbbing away. After a few hours, he began to wonder when they were going to stop. Curious, he asked a native why the drums were going on so long. Rather than reply though, the native ran away screaming with a terrified look on his face. Thinking he had probably broken some taboo by asking an intrusive question, the bloke decided to just forget about the drums and enjoy his holiday. After two days of continuous drumming, broken sleep, mild headaches and so on though, the drums were really starting to get to him. On the beach, he crossed over to a local, a man with his wife and kids, and asked, "When are the drums going to stop?" The native looked at him in horror. All of a sudden, the whole family was backing away, then they turned and fled. The bloke decided to leave it another night, ears stuffed with cotton wool. The next morning though, they were still pounding away in the hills. He went outside, found an old native man, then pounced on him and grabbed him in a vicious headlock. "Listen to me, old man," said the bloke, "You will tell me when the drums stop, or I'll snap your damn neck." The old man looked up at him, shuddering, and said, "I would rather die than be the one who stops the drums." The bloke, perplexed, asked him why. Slowly, reluctantly, the old man said, "You are a foolish young man. When the drums are over, the harmonica solo starts!"

A Russian pianist, a Cuban guitarist, a Scottish piper and an English drummer were sharing a compartment on a train. The Russian, in an attempt to impress the other passengers, said, "In Russia we have so much vodka that we can afford to throw it away." He then pulled out a bottle of fine Russian vodka and, to the dismay of the Scot, threw it out the window. In a spirit of one-upmanship, the Cuban replied, "In Cuba, we have so many cigars that we can simply throw them away," and proceeded to dump a box of the finest Cuban cigars onto the track. Everyone looked at the Scot, who glowered back. He said, "Well, in Britain..." and then grabbed the English drummer and threw him out of the window.

****

What do you call a jazz musician without a girlfriend? Homeless.

****

What's the difference between a coffin and a cello? With the coffin, the corpse is on the inside.

****

What do you call someone who hangs around a bunch of musicians? A drummer.

****

A famous blues musician died. His tombstone bore the inscription "Didn't wake up this morning..."

****

A businessman was interviewing a nervous young woman for a position in his company. He wanted to find out something about her personality, so he asked, "If you could have a conversation with someone living or dead who would it be?" The girl thought about the question: "The living one," she replied.

****

Manager to interviewee: "For this job we need someone who is responsible." Interviewee to manager: "I'm your man then – in my last job, whenever anything went wrong I was responsible."

****

A businessman turned to a colleague during the course of a long lunch and asked, "So, how many do you have working at your office?" His friend shrugged and replied, "Oh, about a third."

****

How long have I been working at that office? As a matter of fact, I've been working there ever since they threatened to sack me.

****

How many company directors does it take to screw in a light bulb? Just one. He holds the bulb and the world revolves around him.

****

Mike was walking through the office when he came across a secretary sitting at her desk, sobbing her eyes out. "Are you alright?" he asked sympathetically. "What's wrong?" She sniffed, and replied, "My boss said that I'm not cute enough to make so many typing errors!"

****

The boss was in a good mood. He walked into the office and cracked a joke he'd heard that morning. The staff all creased up apart from one girl in the corner who just glared at him. "What's up," grumbled the boss, "no sense of humour?" The girl shrugged. "I don't need to laugh.

I finish on Thursday."

****

My boss said that I would get a raise when I'd earned it. He's mad if he thinks I'm going to wait that long.

****

Government studies show that a 7% unemployment level is acceptable to 93% of the population.

****

A motivational speaker was making a speech, but kept getting interrupted. Finally, sick of it, he grabbed the microphone and said loudly, "We seem to have a great many fools here tonight. Would it be possible to hear just one at a time?" Someone at the back of the room laughed nastily, and said, "Yes, good idea. Get on with your speech."

****

A businessman was having a hard time lugging his lumpy, oversized travel bag onto the plane. With the aid of a flight attendant, he finally managed to cram it into the overhead cupboard. "Do you always carry such heavy luggage?" she sighed. "Never again," the man replied.

"Next time, I'm going in the bag."

****

They say that a fool and his money are soon parted. What I'd like to know is how the fool and his money got together in the first place...

****

A bloke was sitting in his garden one afternoon when a lorry pulled up in front of his house. The driver got out of the lorry, walked to the grassy area by to the road, dug a hole, then got back into the truck. A few minutes later, a different chap got out of the passenger seat, walked to the hole, proceeded to fill it back in, and then returned to the lorry. The driver then moved the lorry 50 feet up the road, and the process repeated itself. This went on all up the road. The bloke, who was already a bit upset about the poor quality of the road, couldn't believe his eyes. He stormed down to the lorry, pounded on the window, and demanded to know what was going on. The driver replied, "We're part of a road improvement project. The bloke who plants the trees called in sick."

****

A young woman is getting ready for a shower. She's standing there naked, just about to go in, when there is a knock at the door. "Who is it?" calls the woman. A voice answers, "I'm a blind salesman." The woman thinks it would be quite a thrill to have a blind man in the room while she's naked, so she lets him in. The man walks in, looks up at her, and his jaw drops, then, as a broad grin spreads over his face, he says, "Well, I was going to try to sell you a blind...."

****

A door-to-door vacuum cleaner salesman manages to fast-talk his way into a woman's home in the Scottish highlands. "This machine really is the best ever," he gushes, and tips a bag of dust, dirt and rubbish over the lounge floor. "What the hell are you doing?" shrieks the woman. "Don't worry madam," replies the salesman, "this machine is wonderful. If it doesn't remove all the muck from your carpet, I'll lick it up myself." The woman looks at him, then shrugs and says, "Will you need some ketchup? The electricity won't be back on until Thursday, you see."

****

If the car had followed the same technological curve as the computer, a Rolls-Royce today would cost £50, do a million miles to the litre, and explode once a week, killing everyone nearby.

A doctor, an engineer and a computer scientist were sitting around late one evening, discussing which was the oldest profession. The doctor pointed out that according to the Bible, God created Eve from Adam's rib. This obviously required surgery to obtain the rib, so his was the oldest profession in the world. The engineer countered with an earlier passage in the Bible that stated that God created order from the chaos. That was most certainly the biggest and best engineering project ever, so her profession was the oldest profession. The computer scientist leaned back in her chair, smiled, and responded, "Yes, but who do you think created the chaos?"

✳✳✳✳

Two Irish builders were working on a house. One was on a ladder, nailing planks. He repeatedly reached into his nail pouch, pulled out a nail, looked at it, and either tossed it over his shoulder or proceeded to nail it into the wood. The other one looked up at him, perplexed, and called out, "Why are you throwing some of the nails away?" The first bloke explained, "When I pull the nail out of my bag, it's either pointed towards me or pointed towards the house. I can only use the ones that are pointed towards the house. You can't hammer a nail in flat end first. Do you think I'm stupid?" His mate shook his head, and called back, "Sure and y'are stupid! You shouldn't throw away those nails that are pointed towards you! They're for the other side of the house!"

****

University: A fountain of knowledge where everyone goes to drink.

****

Two Media Studies graduates decided to have a reunion, and they arranged to meet at one's house, in Manchester. The visitor inevitably got lost, so he phoned his friend and said, "Hi, look, I'm on my way over, but I'm lost and I've got no idea where I am." His friend replied, "It's okay, just look at the nearest road junction. There will be a sign. Read it to me." The lost one looked around, and then said, "Oh, okay, I see it. It says 'No Parking'." "Oh good," replied his friend, "you're right down the street. I'll drop by to pick you up."

****

Ice is no longer available in drinks in the Student Union bar at the Agricultural college. The girl who knew the recipe has graduated.

****

A professor was known for being a generous marker. The grades he gave for one of his courses were based solely on two exams, and the stuff on the exams was covered entirely in the textbook. As word of the course spread, each term there was a larger group of students who turned up infrequently, or not at all, just showing up for the exams. Finally, it got so bad that one term, about half of the students never turned up at all until the exams. On the day of the first exam, the students sat down and a graduate assistant handed out the papers, explaining, "The professor is ill, so I'll be taking the exams." When they opened the booklet, the students discovered just one question. It listed twenty grainy staff photos, and the instructions read, "Circle the picture of the professor who teaches this course."

****

University is like a gorgeous woman. You try really hard to get in, then, nine months later, you wish you had never come.

****

Why is a degree like a condom? It's rolled up when you get it, it represents a lot of effort, and it's worthless the next day.

****

A professor is someone who talks in someone else's sleep.

****

When lecturers want your opinion, they'll give it to you.

****

Education boosts your earning capacity. Ask any professor.

****

You should never let your schooling interfere with your education.

****

Did you hear about the couple with three children in University? They're getting poorer by degrees.

****

A student who changes the course of history is probably taking an exam.

****

If you took all the students that fell asleep in lectures and laid them end to end, they'd be a lot more comfortable.

****

While visiting a small primary school, an inspector interviewing the headmistress became irritated at the noise the children were making in the next room. Angrily, he opened the door and grabbed one of the taller girls who seemed to be doing most of the talking. He dragged her into the head's office, ordered her to be absolutely silent, and stood her in the corner. A few minutes later, a small boy stuck his head into the room and begged, "Please, sir, may we have our teacher back?"

****

A science graduate asks, "Why does it work?" An engineering graduate asks, "How does it work?" A business studies graduate asks, "How much will it cost?" A media studies graduate asks, "Do you want fries with that?"

****

One day, a very attractive undergraduate girl visited her professor's office. She pulled the chair closer to the professor, smiled at him shyly, bumped his knee "accidentally", leaned over towards him to fiddle in her bag for a moment, exposing her cleavage, and said, "Professor, I really need to pass your course. It is extremely important to me. It is so important that I'll do anything you suggest." The professor, somewhat taken aback, replied, "Anything?" The undergraduate nodded, and huskily murmured, "Yes, anything you say." After a moment's thought, the professor asked, "What are you doing tomorrow afternoon at 3:30?" The student smiled sexily, and said, "Oh, nothing at all, sir." The professor nodded, then smiled and said, "Excellent! Come to room 15. I'm holding a detailed revision lecture, so bring a notebook."

****

In a huge psychology lecture class, a professor took great pains each lecture to read a chapter of his weighty textbook, written by his good self, to the class. One student made a point of sitting in the front row, right in front of the podium, and knitted while the professor read the text. It irritated the professor no end, so after about five weeks of this, the professor paused mid-lecture, looked at the young lady, and said, "Miss, are you aware that Freud considered knitting to be a form of masturbation?" The student looked up and retorted, "You do it your way Professor – I'll do it mine."

****

An economics lecturer had a strict policy that the fortnightly examinations were to be completed in exactly one hour and anyone who kept writing on their paper after the bell would get a zero. Well, one session a student kept writing on his exam paper for a moment or two after the bell and then confidently strode up to turn it in. The professor looked at him and said, "Don't bother to hand that paper in... you get a zero for continuing after the bell." The bloke looked at him and said, "Professor, do you know who I am?" The professor replied,

"No, and I don't care if your father is Tony Blair... you get a zero on this exam." The bloke, with a enraged look on his face, shouted, "You mean you have no idea who I am?" The professor responded, "No, I've no idea, and I couldn't care less." The bloke grinned, then said, "Good!" quickly whipped his exam into the middle of the stack, and sprinted out.

****

In a courtroom, a mugger was on trial. The victim, asked if she recognised the defendant, said, "Yes, that's him. I saw him clear as day. I'd remember his face anywhere." Unable to contain himself, the defendant burst out with, "She's lying! I was wearing a mask!"

****

A man on trial had pleaded "not guilty". When the jury, eight women and four men, had been seated, and the trial was under way, the defendant switched his plea to "guilty". "Why the change?" asked the judge, "Were you pressured to plead guilty?" "No Your Honour," the man replied, "When I pleaded 'not guilty', I didn't know women would be on the jury. I can't fool even one, so I'll never fool eight of them."

****

When you go to court, just remember that you are trusting your fate to twelve people who weren't clever enough to get out of jury duty!

This bloke happened upon a little antique shop, so he went in and took a look around. Way up on a high shelf he saw a little brass mouse figurine, and he really liked it. He asked the owner how much it was, and she replied, "It's £50 for the mouse, and £100 for the story that goes with it." The bloke thought about it, then handed over fifty quid and said, "I'll just take the statue, thanks." He walked out with the mouse. As he was walking home, he noticed the figurine was hollow, with two little holes. Holding it up to his mouth, it made a melodious whistle. No sooner had he started than he was being followed by three little mice. When he stopped, they stopped. When he turned left, they turned left. "That's strange," thought the bloke. As he continued walking, the mice were joined by more mice, until the bloke looked like the Pied Piper, leading a huge procession of mice. Spooked out, he ran over to the side of a nearby canal and flung the statue into the water. The mice leaped over the edge and down into the water, following the statue, and drowned. In a bit of a daze, the bloke went back to the antique shop. When he walked through the door, the owner gave him a smug smile and said, "So, you've come back to hear the story?" The bloke shook his head. "No. As a matter of fact, I was wondering if you had any little brass lawyers."

****

A witness was called to the stand to testify about a head-on car crash. "Whose fault was this accident?" one lawyer asked. "As near as I could tell," replied the witness, "they hit each other at about the same time."

****

In the courtroom, the prosecutor thundered at the defendant, "Did you kill the victim?" The defendant shook his head, and replied, "No, I did not." "Do you know what the penalties are for perjury?" asked the lawyer. "Yes, I do," replied the defendant. "They're a hell of a lot better than the penalty for murder."

****

A policeman broke up a scuffle outside a pub. "He started it!" said one man, infuriated. "It's not my fault!" replied the other. "Perhaps you could tell me what happened, Gents," said the policeman. "He kicked me in the bollocks!" accused the first man. "I didn't mean to," replied the second. "How was I supposed to know you were about to turn round?"

****

A zombie popped down to his local brains shop to get some brain for supper. The sign boasted about the quality of the professional brain sold there, so he asked the butcher, "How much is it for Doctor's brain?" "That's £3 an ounce." The zombie nodded, and asked, "How about Engineer's brain?" "£4 an ounce, sir." "What about lawyer's brain?" "Ah," replied the butcher, "that's £100 an ounce." The zombie was aghast. "Why is lawyer's brain so much more?" The butcher looked at him. "Do you have any idea how many lawyers you need to kill to get one ounce of brain?"

****

A primary school teacher was asking students what their parents did for a living. "John, you first," she said. "What does your mother do all day?" John stood up and said, "She's a doctor." "That's wonderful," said the teacher. "How about you, Amy?" Amy shyly stood up, scuffed her feet and said, "My father is a mailman." The teacher smiled, and said, "That's lovely. Thank you, Amy. What about your father, Billy?" Billy proudly stood up and announced, "My dad is a pimp at the local brothel." The teacher was horrified, and promptly changed the subject. Later that day, at lunchtime, she went round to Billy's house and rang the bell. His father answered the door. The teacher explained what his son had said and demanded an explanation. The man sighed, and said, "Actually, I'm a libel lawyer, but how do you explain a thing like that to a seven-year-old?"

A lawyer died and went to heaven. When he arrived before the pearly gates, a chorus of angels began to sing in his honour and St. Peter himself came out to shake his hand. "Mr Wilson," said St. Peter, "it is a great honour to have you here at last. At 1028 years, you've broken Methuselah's record." "What are you talking about?" asked the lawyer, puzzled. "I'm 56. Well, I was 56 anyway." St. Peter was surprised. "56? But aren't you John Wilson?" "Yes." "A lawyer?" "Yes." "From 23, Acacia Gardens, Wimbledon?" "Yes." "Let me check the records," said St Peter, and his eyes unfocussed. Suddenly, he slapped his hand against his forehead. "I see! Someone totalled your billing hours!"

****

A lawyer died in poverty and many barristers of the city subscribed to a fund for his funeral. The Lord Chief Justice was asked to donate a pound. "Only a pound?" said the Justice, "Only a pound to bury a lawyer? Here's twenty quid; go and bury a few more of them."

****

A kind woman died. At her funeral were her doctor, her accountant and her lawyer. Each had promised her that they would put £100 into her coffin before she was cremated. The doctor went up, said farewell, and placed his money in the coffin. The accountant then went up, said farewell and placed his money into the coffin. Finally, the lawyer went up, took the £200 out of the coffin, and dropped a cheque for £300 in its place.

****

A bloke was charged with stealing a car. After a long trial, he was acquitted by the jury. Later that day, the bloke came back to the judge who had presided at the hearing. "Your honour," he said, "I want that damn lawyer of mine arrested." "Why?" asked the judge, surprised. "He got you off. What do you want to have him arrested for?" "Well, your honour," replied the bloke, "I didn't have any money to pay his fee, so he went and took the car I stole."

****

"You seem to be displaying an unusual level of intelligence for a man of your background," sneered a lawyer at the witness. "If I wasn't sworn under oath," replied the witness, "I'd return the compliment."

****

A lawyer is a man who helps you get what's coming to him.

****

Little Katy turned to her mother as they were walking through a graveyard and asked, "Mummy, do they ever bury two people in the same grave?" "Of course not, dear," replied her mother, "Why would you think that?" "That tombstone back there said 'Here lies a lawyer and an honest man.'"

****

The defendant who pleads his own case has a fool for a client, but at least he knows that his lawyer won't be ripping him off.

****

God decided to take the devil to court and settle their differences once and for all. When Lucifer heard the news, he laughed and said, "Where does the old fool think he's going to find a lawyer?"

****

It has been discovered that lawyers are the larval stage of politicians.

****

There is no better way to exercise your imagination and creativity than to study the law.

A small town that cannot support one lawyer can always support two.

****

There are two kinds of lawyers – those who know the law, and those who know the judge.

****

At a convention of biologists, one researcher remarked to another, "Did you know that in our lab we have switched from rats to lawyers for our experiments?" "Really?" the other replied, "Why did you switch?" "Well, there were five reasons. First, we found that lawyers are far more plentiful. Second, the lab assistants don't get so attached to them. Third, lawyers multiply faster. Fourth, animal rights groups do not object to their torture. Finally, fifth, there are some things even a rat won't do. There is one big drawback, however – it can be very hard to project the test results to relate to human beings."

****

A lawyer's dog, running about unattended, heads straight for a butcher shop and runs off with a big joint of meat. The butcher, recognising the dog, goes to lawyer's office and asks, "If a dog running unleashed steals a piece of meat from my shop, do I have a right to demand payment for the meat from the dog's owner?" The lawyer nods, and replies, "Absolutely." The butcher smiles, and says "Then you owe me £14.23. Your dog got loose, and stole a joint from me earlier." The lawyer nods, and writes the butcher a cheque for £14.23. The next morning, the butcher opened his post and found a letter from the lawyer. Inside was an invoice – £100 for consultation without appointment.

When a lawyer tells a client that he has a sliding fee schedule, what he means is that after he invoices you, it's hard to get back on your financial feet.

It was so cold last winter that I saw a lawyer with his hands in his own pockets.

An old lady paid a solicitor for an appointment to sort out her will with a £50 note. As she was leaving, the solicitor realised that there was a second £50 note stuck to the back. He suddenly found himself wrestling with an urgent ethical problem. "Do I tell my accountant?"

At the turn of the century, a respectable western lawyer was filing some insurance papers when he came to a question which asked, "If your father is dead, state the cause." Unwilling to reveal that his father had been hanged for cattle rustling, the lawyer evaded the problem by answering, "He died taking part in a public ceremony; he was killed when the platform gave way."

****

After successfully passing the necessary exams, a man opened his own law firm. He was sitting at his desk when his secretary came in to inform him that a Mr. Jones had arrived to see him. "Show him in," the lawyer replied. As Mr. Jones was being ushered in, the lawyer picked up the phone and declared into it, "And you can tell them that we won't accept less then fifty thousand pounds. Don't even call me until you can agree to that amount!" Slamming the phone down, he stood up and greeted Mr. Jones. "Good Morning, Mr. Jones. What can I do for you?" Mr. Jones smiled, and said, "I work for BT. I'm here to connect your phones."

****

Experts are people who know a lot about very little, and who go along learning more and more about less and less until they know everything about nothing. Lawyers, on the other hand, are people who know very little about many things, and keep learning less and less about more and more until they know practically nothing about everything. Judges are people who start out knowing everything about everything, but end up knowing nothing about anything, because of their constant association with experts and lawyers.

****

An airliner was having engine trouble and the pilot instructed the cabin crew to have the passengers take their seats and prepare for an emergency landing. A few minutes later, the pilot asked the air hostess if everyone was buckled in and ready. "All ready back here, Captain," came the reply, "except for one lawyer, who is still passing out business cards."

****

A gang of robbers broke into a lawyer's club by mistake. The old legal lions gave them a fight for their lives, and the gang was lucky to escape. "It ain't so bad," one crook noted when the gang got back to their den. "We got out with £50." "I warned you to stay clear of lawyers!" the boss screamed. "We had over £270 when we broke in!"

****

A man went into a police station in a small town, obviously desperate. He asked the bloke at the desk, "Is there a criminal lawyer in town?"

The policeman nodded, and replied, "Yes, but we can't prove it yet."

****

Talk is cheap – until lawyers get involved.

****

Did you hear about the terrorist that hijacked an aeroplane full of lawyers? He threatened to release one every hour if his demands weren't met.

****

There was a doctor who refused to pay the rent on his outdoor toilet. He didn't like the lawyer living downstairs.

****

What do a lawyer and a sperm have in common? Both have something like a one in 3 million chance of becoming a human being.

****

The best place to find a good lawyer is in the graveyard.

****

The difference between a lawyer and a whore is that a whore only
screws one person at a time.

****

Sporting Triumphs

7

Jokes about Sport

Two blokes were out playing golf. "Did you hear about William Rogers?" asked one. "No," said the other curiously, "what about him?" "Well," said the first one, "he went mad last Saturday and beat his wife to death with a golf club." The other one shuddered. "God, that's awful." They paused for a moment's reflection, and then the other asked, "How many strokes?"

****

Two blokes are out at the sixth, teeing off. The first makes a reasonable drive but the second gives it a tremendous wallop. Ahead, on the fairway, a groundsman wanders out and into the path of the ball. It hits him square on the temple, and he collapses. The two golfers rush up, but find the guy dead, with the ball lodged in the side of his skull. There's blood everywhere. "Oh, Christ, no!" yells the second guy, "what am I going to do?" The first guy looks at him. "Come on, it's not that bad. A pitching wedge has the loft to get that free."

****

An accountant has been working for a billionaire client for 25 years. To celebrate the event, the billionaire says he'd like to get the accountant a present, so the accountant asks for a set of golf clubs. "How many are in a set?" asks the billionaire. "Basically 14," replies the accountant. "Should be able to do that," says the rich man. A month passes, and the accountant is starting to wonder if perhaps he should have been more modest and asked for a watch, when the billionaire calls again. "I've got you some golf clubs," says the billionaire. "Thank you!" says the accountant, "It's really very generous and..." "Hell," says the billionaire, cutting him off, "it's nothing. I wasn't even able to get you a full set, just the ten. It's worse than that, too. Only six of them have hotels within the grounds."

****

A policeman called a bloke in to question him about his wife's death. "Could you tell me what happened?" he asked. "Well," said the bloke, "I didn't realise my wife was at the red tee getting ready to swing. I drove off, and the ball struck her in the head." The policeman nodded, and said, "That agrees with the coroner's report, but I have another question. Why did she also have a golf ball up her arse?" The bloke shrugged. "Oh, that was my mulligan."

****

Two golfers were playing near the edge of the course. One of them looked over the fence in amazement and said, "Look! Those idiots over there are out skating on the pond in this blizzard!"

The real reason men like to go fishing is that it's the only time anyone will ever say to them, "Oh my God, that's a big one!"

****

What's the difference between Middlesborough FC and a triangle? A triangle's got three points.

****

Do you know why they called it golf? Well, all the other four-letter words were taken...

****

A keen golfer was sometimes accompanied by his wife. On one particular afternoon he was having a disastrous time. Teeing off on the 14th he pulled his shot so badly it spun off towards a groundsman's hut. Unfortunately, the hut was obstructing the line. However, his wife, who was along that day, noticed that the hut had two doors, and it was possible that if both doors were opened he would be able to play through. Of course, he asked his wife to go round the back and open the far door. When she did, sure enough, there was a clear path through to the green, although the ball needed to keep flat. He pulled out a wood, lined up and took the shot. As the ball cracked off his wife, curious, looked round the doorway. Tragically, the ball hit her in the centre of the forehead, killing her stone dead. Well, a few weeks later the widower was playing the same course with a friend. Again, he pulled his shot at the 14th, and ended up in front of the hut. "Hey, you might be able to play through if we opened both doors," observed the friend. The bloke shuddered and went pale. "No way. Very bad memories. Last time I did that, I ended up with a seven."

****

Three blokes assembled for a round of golf on Mothering Sunday. All were quite surprised at having been able to escape from the family for the day, and so they compared notes on how they managed it. The first bloke said, "I bought my wife a dozen red roses, and she was so surprised and touched that she let me go." The second guy said, "Yeah. I bought my wife a diamond ring, and she was so thrilled that she let me go." The third guy shook his head, and said, "I woke up this morning, farted thunderously, scratched my arse, then turned to my wife, belched and said, 'Golf course or intercourse?' She blinked and replied, 'I'll put your clubs in the car.'"

****

Why doesn't Mexico have an Olympic team? Because everybody who can run, jump and swim is already in the U.S.

Boxing is a lot like ballet. Except, of course, that there's no music, no choreography, and the dancers punch each other. All-in wrestling, however, is exactly like ballet...

****

A golfer was practising at the driving range after work one evening. He got a large bucket of balls from the kiosk and worked his way through them, but couldn't correct the slice he was trying to iron out. He didn't have the cash for a second bucket of balls, and as he was alone at the range he decided to go and scavenge some, so he walked up the edge of the range collecting balls from bushes and weeds, trying to be inconspicuous. To be able to carry more, he loaded the big, deep pockets of his baggy trousers. Walking back to the tee, he noticed a pretty young woman who had started practising. When he got closer, he saw that she was staring at the strange-shaped bulges in his groin. A bit embarrassed, he explained to her: "Um...they're just golf balls." She looked at him with a mix of sympathy and awe, and said, "That's like tennis elbow, yeah?"

****

Three blokes arrived late at the ski resort, and when they got to the hotel found that they'd have to share a room until the morning, because nothing else was available. When they got up there they found it just had one large bed. "It's just for one night," they thought,

251

and went to bed. The next morning, the one on the far right said, "I had a really odd dream last night. I kept dreaming that I was wanking like a furious donkey, but I couldn't feel my hands." "That's really strange," said the bloke on the far right, "because that's what I dreamt, too. Exactly the same. Eerie." "You lads!" laughed the guy in the middle. "I just dreamt I was skiing..."

****

A man was walking down a street in Brazil when he heard a woman screaming and noticed a smell of burning. He ran round the corner to find a huge crowd of people watching a building burn and wringing their hands. On the eighth floor, a woman was leaning out of a window screaming for someone to save her baby. The man stepped forward and called, "Throw down your baby. I'll catch her." The woman yelled back, "No! You'll drop her, and she'll die!" "No, I won't," shouted back the man. "I'm the goalkeeper for the Brazilian national team. I've played every international for ten years. I've never missed a match, and I've never let in a goal. I'm not going to drop your baby." The woman was incredulous. "You've never let in even one goal?" "No, never," he calls back. "I am the greatest goalkeeper the world has ever seen. Throw down your baby." And with that he went into a crouch, legs bent, body angling forward, arms ready. The woman looked at the flames licking up the building, realised she had no choice, shouted, "Okay, here she comes!" and with a shriek threw her baby down. Unfortunately, as she did so, she knocked her elbow against the window frame, jerking it, and the baby went flying, tumbling wildly off-course. The crowd gasped, the woman screamed, but the man never took his eye off the baby. He stayed dead still as the child fell, watching it tumble and spin, until it was just feet from the pavement. Suddenly, like a panther, he leapt across the street, a jump of 25 feet, snatched the child from the air, rolled and came up with the baby clutched to his chest. He looked around at the crowd, acknowledged their admiration, and lifted an arm to the woman in a salute. Then he turned and, in one swift motion, drop-kicked the baby through a plate-glass window and into the back of a hardware shop.

****

A very rich bloke wanted to give his sons presents, so he called them to him and asked them what they wanted. The oldest son asked for a train set, so his father purchased London Underground for him. The second asked for a CD player, so his father bought him Virgin Radio. The final son wanted a cowboy outfit, so his father gave him Everton.

****

A poor golfer was having a bad round. He was 30 over par after four holes, had lost 14 balls in the same piece of water and had practically ploughed the rough trying to get a ball out. Then, on the green of the fifth, his caddy coughed just as he took a ten-inch putt, and he sliced it. The golfer went wild. "By God! You've got to be the worst damn caddy in the whole wide world!" The caddy looked at him sourly, and replied, "I doubt it. That would be too much of a coincidence."

****

A keen golfer was granted an audience with the Pope on a visit to the Vatican. When he got to see the pontiff, he kissed the hem of his robe and said, "Holiness, I have a question that only you can answer. Is there a golf course in heaven?" The Pope blessed the man, and replied, "My son, I do not know the answer to your question, as I do not play golf. But I will ask God for you, and pass on his answer." The next morning the man was awoken, feeling a bit groggy, at seven in the morning, by a hotel porter bringing him a note. It was from the Pope himself, and read: "My son, Heaven has the most fantastic golf course. It is eternally in perfect condition, the weather is ideal and the greens play like a dream. I'm afraid you're booked in to tee off at 11 o'clock this morning, however."

****

A guy out on the golf course takes a high speed ball right in the crotch. Writhing in agony, he falls to the ground. As soon as he could manage, he took himself to the doctor. He said, "How bad is it doc? I'm going on my honeymoon next week and my fiancée is still a virgin in every way." The doctor told him, "I'll have to put your penis in a splint to let it heal and keep it straight. It should be okay next week." So he took four tongue depressors and formed a neat little 4-sided bandage, and wired it all together; an impressive work of art. The guy mentions none of this to his girl, marries and goes on their honeymoon. That night in the motel room she rips open her blouse to reveal a gorgeous set of breasts. This was the first time he saw them. She said, "You're the first, no one has ever touched these breasts." He drops his pants and says, "Look at this, it's still in the CRATE!"

****

This bloke was a passionate fisherman, and spent all weekend at the waterside regardless of the weather. One Sunday he headed off to the riverside as usual. However, it was freezing cold and pouring with rain and, uncharacteristically, he decided to go home. When he got back, he noticed that his wife was still in bed, so he made a cup of coffee for the two of them, went up to the bedroom and said, "Hello, darling. I've made some coffee. It's really dreadful out there, freezing cold and lashing with rain." "Yeah," she said sleepily, "and that stupid bloody husband of mine went fishing anyway!"

****

The Irish parachutist realised that he had problems when his snorkel wouldn't open.

"I have a confession, love," a bloke said to his new wife. "I'm a golf-player. Much as I love you, you're not going to see me at weekends during the golfing season, I'm afraid." "That's OK," she replied, "I have a confession too. I'm a hooker." "No problem," replied the bloke. "Just keep your head down and straighten your left arm."

****

Two Scotsmen, Jim and Freddie, were out playing golf, and they decided to put some competition into the game by putting money on the round - 50p. Well, with such a sum at stake both men were concentrating fiercely, and they were perfectly matched for the first nine holes. On the tenth, though, Jim drove into the rough and couldn't find his ball. He called Freddie over to help and the pair searched around. Finally, desperate to avoid the four-stroke penalty for a lost ball, Jim popped a new ball out of his pocket when Freddie wasn't looking. "Freddie lad, I've found the ball," said Jim. "You filthy, cheating swine!" exploded Freddie. "I never thought that any friend of mine would stoop so low as to cheat in a game that had money on it!" "I'm not cheating!" protested Jim, "I've found my ball, and I'll play it where it lies." "That's not your ball," sneered Freddie. "I've been standing on your ball for the last five minutes!"

Two Irish blokes were out hunting ducks. Despite a whole day of vigorous hunting, though, they completely failed to harm even one duck. Finally, one turned to the other and said, "Maybe we'd do better if we threw that dog a bit higher."

A bloke was walking his three-legged greyhound through a park when he spotted something in the undergrowth. Going for a closer look he found that it was a lamp, so he gave it a quick buffing on the off-chance and out popped a genie. "Oh, hello," said the genie. "I suppose you want a wish?" The bloke nodded, too surprised to speak. "Well, you can have the one." "Alright," said the bloke. "Um...can you fix it so my dog will win all six races one evening at the dog races? They'll put ludicrous odds on it, because he's three-legged, and I can put my life savings on and be a rich man." The genie looked doubtful and said, "Well, I dunno. I mean, a three-legged dog winning six races is a pretty obvious sign of supernatural intervention, and things are supposed to be more subtle than that, according to the Codes and Regulations For Supernatural Semi-Divinities Act 1941. Can't you think of anything else?" "Well, I suppose so," said the bloke. "I'm a Southampton fan, so could you fix it so we win the Premiership this year?" The genie sighed. "About that dog of yours..."

****

Two blokes were on an African safari when they came across some lion tracks. Suddenly nervous, one said to the other, "You follow these forward and find out where the lion's got to. I'll follow them backward, and find out where it's been..."

A poor golfer spent the day at an expensive country golf club courtesy of a rich friend, playing badly and enjoying the luxury of a caddy. By the time he got to the 18th he was 88 over par. Seeing a pond over past the green, he said to the caddy, "I've played so badly today that I'm tempted to go and drown myself in that lake." The caddy looked back at him and said, "To be frank, I find it difficult to believe that Sir could keep his head down long enough."

****

If at first you don't succeed, BASE jumping is not your sport.

****

Why did God invent golf? So men had an excuse to dress like pimps.

****

In Africa, some of the tribes have a peculiar custom of beating the ground with clubs and uttering unearthly cries. Anthropologists have described this as a form of demonic exorcism. In Europe, we call it golf.

****

Have you ever thought about which game came first? Tennis has often been suggested, because the Old Testament states, "Joseph served in Pharaoh's Court." Others prefer the cricket hypothesis, because Genesis itself starts with "In the big Inning." There's no doubt about the last game that will ever be played, though. It's bridge. At the end of the world, we are told, "Gabriel will play the last trump..."

****

In the mornings, directors talk about golf in their offices. In the afternoons, they talk about work on the golf course...

****

Two alien scientists visited Earth to examine local customs. When they met to pool their knowledge the first alien told of a peculiar religious ceremony it had seen, of impressive magical power. "I went to a large green arena shaped like a meteorite crater. Several thousand worshippers were gathered around the outside. Two priests walked to the centre of the field, where a rectangular area was marked, and hammered six spears into the ground, three at each end, then linked the spears in each set of three with small tubes. Then 11 more priests came out, clad in white robes. Finally, two high priests wielding clubs walked to the centre area. One of the white-robed priests produced a red orb and hurled it at the ones with the clubs." "Wow," replied the other alien, "what happened next?" The first alien said, "Every time they performed the ceremony, at this point it began to rain!"

✱✱✱✱

Three friends were getting ready to play golf when a bloke walked down the path to the first hole and asked if he could join them. They agreed, and began golfing. The new guy played left-handed, and shot a wonderful round. After they finished, the fourth golfer was invited back the following week. "I'd love to, thanks," he said, "But I might be a little late." The next week, he turned up on time and again shot a great round, but to everyone else's surprise, he was playing right-handed. Again he was invited back, and again he said. "I'd love to, thanks, but I might be a little late." The following week he again turned up on time and played left-handed. He played another good round, and when he was asked back another time, replied, "I'd love to, thanks, but I might be a little late." Well, he was on time again, played left-handed again, and got another good round in. When he was invited back to his now-regular slot, he again warned the others that he might be a little late. Unable to bear it any longer, one of the three friends asked him: "We've seen you play superbly both left- and right-handed, which I think is fantastic, and you always tell us you might be late. Why is that?" The golfer responded, "Well, like many players, I'm superstitious. When I wake up to go golfing, I look at my wife. If she's sleeping on her left side, I golf left-handed. If she's sleeping on her right side, I golf right-handed. If she's on her back; well, I'm going to be a little late..."

****

"When you go diving," warned the Caribbean instructor, "always take a friend with you. If you run out of air, your friend can help you. If you forget which way the surface is - I know it sounds silly, but it's easy - your friend can help you. If you have equipment problems, your friend can help you. Most important of all, though, is that if a shark turns up, your chance of survival is 50%, not 0!"

****

The manager of Reading Football Club was woken up by a call from his local police station. "I'm afraid the club has been broken into, sir." Horrified, the manager asked, "Did they get the cups?" "No, sir," replied the policeman, "they didn't go into the kitchen."

A parachutist who always carried his parachute as hand luggage had checked in for a commercial flight to the States and was entering the departure lounge. At the X-ray machine, the inspector did not recognise the 'chute, and insisted that the bloke unpack it to prove he wasn't hiding anything in there. They argued over it for a while, and eventually the supervisor came over, calmed the bloke and the inspector down and let the bloke go on his way. Later, on the plane, he found that he was sitting next to an old couple who had seen him at the X-ray machine. The old boy turned to his wife and said, "Ellie dear, that young man has a parachute in his backpack," and pointed to where the bloke had placed his 'chute under the seat. The old woman looked doubtful, turned to the parachutist and asked, "Is that really a parachute?" Still irritated by the inspector, the bloke turned to her and said, "Yes, of course. Did you not get yours?"

****

Why do mountain climbers rope themselves together? It's to stop anyone who accidentally comes to his or her senses from going home.

****

A Scot and a Yank were talking about golf. "In most parts of the United States we can't play in winter. We have to wait until the spring," said the American. "Och, ye big softies," replied the Scot. "Surely ye can play if ye put a will to it? We dinnae let the snow and cold fess us." The Yank looked doubtful. "Well, what do you do, paint your balls black?" he asked. "No," replied the surprised Scot. "We'll just put on a thick pair of thermal troosers."

****

Two blokes were out fishing. One of them was making a cast when a stunningly beautiful young woman ran past, stark naked, laughing. Well, it put him off his cast, but he let the matter slip. As he was about to cast again two men in white coats pounded past, neck and neck, grinning. They were less of a distraction, and he was almost ready to cast again when a third bloke ran past, panting desperately, carrying a heavy bucket of sand in each hand. Unable to bear it any longer, the fisherman called to the bloke in the next bay: "Sorry, mate, but do you have any idea what was going on there?" The guy nodded. "There's a nut-house just through those woods. Once a week, regular as clockwork, that woman escapes, rips off all her clothes and runs around the lake. Those three blokes in the white coats are care nurses. They have a race to see which of them can catch her first. The winner intercepts her, and carries her back to the mental home. Occasionally, she insists on having wild sex with her captor before she'll go back." "What about the buckets of sand?" asked the first bloke. "Well," replied his informant, "that's the one who caught her last week. The buckets of sand are his handicap."

Do you know that sport in the Olympics where you track through deep snow, stop to shoot your gun, and then continue? Most of the world calls it the biathlon. In America though, they refer to it as 'winter'...

Sleeping with a woman never harmed any professional footballer. It's staying up all night hunting for a woman to sleep with that does the damage...

Fishermen are proud of their rods.

BASE jumping is an excellent way to relax. It really takes your mind off your problems...

You know that you've been watching too much all-in wrestling when the top of your wardrobe has footprints on it from where you've been jumping off the ropes.

A rugby player was jailed for six months for biting an opponent's ear off. The judge ruled that this action was "not within the normal give-and-take that the sport allows"!

****

After Dinner

8

Jokes about Restaurants and Food

A Polish restaurant was in the habit of putting buckets of shit around the edges of the dining-room to draw the flies away from the diners. The air was so polluted anyway that the smell didn't really make an impact. They had to stop, though. They found that their customers kept getting drunk and eating everything in sight...

****

I ate in a Chinese restaurant a few days ago. It was appalling. I called the waiter over and yelled at him, "This bloody chicken is rubbery!" He smiled at me, and yelled back: "Thank you berry much!"

****

What is the most common speech impediment? Chewing gum.

****

There are four classes of food: Instant, Fast, Frozen and Snack. Within those four classes, the food is broken up into the five different types of nutritional value: Fat, Salt, Caffeine, Sugar and Chocolate.

****

This bloke was having chicken noodle soup in a restaurant. The food arrived, he started tucking in, and then hit a hair. Well, he choked for a while, then called the waitress over and said, "Take this away. There's a hair in it. It's disgusting; I'm not paying for it." Well, the waitress wasn't very happy about this, and the two of them got into an argument over it. Eventually, the bloke stormed out, leaving the soup unpaid-for and an expensive steak going cold in the hatch. Opening the door to yell after him, the waitress saw him going into a brothel down the road, so ten minutes later she nipped out and followed the guy into the brothel. She dashed in while the madam's back was turned, went upstairs and burst into the room where the bloke was. As she had hoped, he was up to his ears in the whore's muff. "You arsehole!" the waitress yelled at him, "you wouldn't eat our damn soup because of a hair, and now look at you!" Unperturbed, the guy turned to the waitress and said, "Yes, and if I find a noodle in here I won't be paying this lady, either."

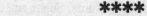

This mushroom girl was gushing to one of her pals about a new boyfriend. "Oh, Lucy," she said, "He's such a fun guy..."

****

As Sid sat down to a big plate of chips and gravy down the local pub a mate of his came over and said, "Here, Sid, me old pal, I thought you were trying to get into shape? And here you are with a high-fat meal and a pint of stout!" Sid looked up and replied, "I am getting into shape. The shape I've chosen is a sphere."

****

"Waiter, I distinctly remembering asking for bread with my meal." "Yes, sir. It's in the sausages, sir."

****

This bloke in a restaurant calls to the waiter, "Excuse me. I can't eat this meal you've just served me." The waiter, shocked, comes over and says, "I'm dreadfully sorry, sir. What's the matter?" The bloke looked at him. "You haven't given me a knife and fork yet!"

****

The other day, I dropped a piece of bread and it fell butter-side up. I was dreadfully shocked, until I realised what had happened - like an idiot, I'd buttered the wrong side.

In a particularly callous and heartless move, the owners of a large mail order diet pill business with tens of thousands of clients sold their mailing list to the boss of a quality chocolate company which was preparing a mailing. The chocolate company's sales rose immediately by 400%; a few weeks later, so did the diet pill company's sales.

****

The most exciting part of a bulimic's birthday party is the bit when the cake leaps out of the girl!

****

This bloke had a nasty accident in a fish-and-chip shop, and tipped some vinegar into his earhole. He now has a bad case of pickled hearing!

****

A bloke was in a restaurant, trying to plough his way through a revolting meal. After a little while he called the waiter over and said: "Waiter, bring the chef out here. I want to complain about the quality of this disgusting muck you've served me." The waiter looked apologetic. "I'm afraid you'll have to wait for half an hour, sir. He's just popped out to get something to eat."

****

This woman was ordering a meal. "I'd like the lamb chops, please - and make them lean, would you?" "Certainly, madam," replied the waiter. "In which direction?"

****

A man and a woman were eating in a swanky restaurant. Their waitress, taking another order at a table a few feet away, noticed the man slowly sliding down his chair and under the table. The woman dining across from him appeared calm and unruffled, apparently unaware that her companion had disappeared. Wanting to make sure that no monkey business was going on the waitress finished taking her order, crossed over to the table and said to the woman, "Pardon me, madam, but I believe your husband just slid under the table." The woman calmly looked up, shook her head and replied, "No, he didn't. As a matter of fact he just walked in, and is heading in this direction..."

****

A Polish couple went into a restaurant and ordered their food. When it was served a few minutes later, the husband started tucking in ravenously while his wife just watched, not touching her food. After a little while the waitress came over and asked, "Is something wrong?"

"I'm waiting for my husband to finish," said the woman. The waitress looked at her and said: "But your dinner's getting cold. You don't need to wait." The woman nodded vigorously. "Yes, I must. It's his turn to go first with our false teeth."

****

"Waiter, there's a flea in my soup!" "Don't worry sir, I'll tell him to hop it."

****

A Scotsman and a Jew were arguing over who could make 20p go further. They decided to give it a try and meet up later to compare notes. When they got back together again, the Jew said, "Well, I used my 20p to buy two cigarettes off a tramp. The first day I smoked one and saved the ashes. The second day I smoked the other and saved the ashes. On the third day I ate the cigarette-butts and used the ashes I'd saved to fertilise my plants." "Ah, you were robbed," replied the Scot smugly. "I used my 20p to buy a black pudding from the butcher. The first day I slit open the casing, scooped out half of the pudding and ate it. The second day I scooped out the other half and ate that. The third day I crapped into the empty black pudding skin. I then took it back to the butcher and said, 'This black pudding smells like shit!' He agreed, and gave me my 20p back!"

****

This bloke was in a curry house, flicking through the menu and idly munching on poppadoms. After a few minutes he called the waiter over. "Waiter, could you possibly explain something on the menu to me?" "Oh, most certainly, sir," replied the waiter cheerfully. "I know Indian food pretty well," said the bloke, "but I've never heard of this dish here, Lamb Tarka. Surely you mean Lamb Tikka?" The waiter shook his head and said, "No sir, we mean Lamb Tarka. It is very similar indeed to Lamb Tikka, you are most correct, but it's just a little 'otter."

****

We reserve the right to serve refuse to anyone.

****

An Indian chef was sacked for being divisive after a week in his new job. He keep favouring curry.

****

A couple of lads had a go at using pickles for a ping-pong game. They found themselves in The Volley of the Dills...

****

Eat a prune! Start a movement!

****

An Irish bloke walked into a café and ordered a big mug of tea. When it arrived he carefully spooned ten teaspoons of sugar slowly into the tea and then started sipping it gently, leaving all the sugar on the bottom. Puzzled, the waitress asked him, "I know it's none of my business, sir, but why didn't you stir your tea?" The bloke looked at her, smiled, and replied, "Well now my lass, I don't like sweet tea."

****

There was a bloke who was absolutely devoted to baked beans. He ate them at every chance he got. He adored them. He even found himself dreaming about them. Unfortunately, they were not as fond of him as he was of them, and they always had a vicious reaction, making him fart like an elephant. One day he met a girl, and they fell in love. As their relationship deepened, he came to understand that they would be married, and he thought to himself, "She's a sweet and gentle girl. She'd never understand me farting all the time like a platoon of troopers," and realising how much it would embarrass and humiliate her he decided to do the only thing he could - he gave up the baked beans. Shortly afterwards they were married. Some months later his car broke down, and, working in a village not that far from his home, he decided to walk home, there not being any taxis. He called his wife and explained that he'd be an hour or two later for dinner because of the breakdown. As he left his office, he thought, "I'll just pop in and grab a quick snack at the café round the corner, to fortify myself for the journey." But when he got inside, the scent of baked beans overwhelmed him. He thought about it, and decided that he'd be able to walk the effects off on the way home, and he'd been so good for so long, and so he'd treat himself, just this once. Next thing he knew, he'd eaten four platefuls of beans. Even as he was leaving the café he could feel the effects; he barely made it out of the door before letting off a fart that rattled the window-panes. He farted constantly all the way home. Two hours later, he was feeling fairly confident that he'd farted his last. He knocked on the door and his wife rushed out, hugged him impulsively and said, "Oh, I'm so glad to see you, darling. I have the most wonderful surprise for you for dinner tonight." He smiled, kissed her, and then she blindfolded him, led him by the hand to the table and sat him down. She was about to remove the blindfold when the phone rang. "I'll just be a moment, love," she told him. "Now wait there, and don't you dare touch that blindfold!" She dashed into the hall and closed the door. As she did so, a terrible spasm rippled through his intestines - the beans' final message to his bottom. Thanking God that his wife was in the hall, he eased his weight onto one buttock and farted. It was a legendary thing; a fart from the pages of history itself. It started off slow and squeaky, then rapidly grew in volume as it dropped in pitch, becoming so thunderous that the table rattled. It went on and on and on, for over 30 seconds. It stank like the very Pit itself, too; thick and sulphurous, with the sickly-sweet odour of rotting fruit. It was enough to make him gag silently, and he'd been used to his own wind for a long time. Grinning in amazement, he grabbed his napkin from the table, and started fanning the air to disperse this astonishing last stand before his wife got back. The last vestiges of the stench were just fading five minutes later when she came back from the hall, and apologised for taking so long. "Did you peek, darling?" she asked him. He smiled, and assured her that he had not moved a muscle. She went round behind him, hugged him and whipped off the blindfold. "You're going to be a father," she gushed, "and everyone's come round to celebrate." His parents, his wife's parents, the vicar and his wife, the local GP, her husband and his boss and her husband all stared back at him, reproachfully.

****

"Waiter, there's a dead beetle in my soup." "Yes, sir, they're dreadful swimmers."

****

This bloke was in a café. He took a big swig out of his mug of coffee and spat it out. "Waiter!" he called, "This is disgusting. This coffee tastes like soap." The waiter rushed over. "I'm dreadfully sorry, sir! I've given you a mug of tea by mistake! I'll bring you a coffee at once.

It tastes like glue."

****

Did you hear about the man who drowned in a bowl of muesli? He was dragged under by a strong currant.

****

Most Japanese do not know that the English have their own word for sushi. We call it 'bait'.

****

If a vegetarian eats vegetables, what does a humanitarian eat?

****

This bloke was in a restaurant and the waiter brought him his meal in a nosebag. "What's the meaning of this?" asked the man indignantly. "Oh, sorry, sir," said the waiter, "I must have misunderstood. The chef told me that you come in every Tuesday and eat like a horse."

****

Despite what many people think, eating oysters will actually improve your sex life. When you eat an oyster, members of the opposite sex feel safe in the knowledge that you'll eat anything.

****

"Waiter, you're not fit to serve a pig!" "I'm doing my best, sir."

****

This bloke walked into a fast-food restaurant, went up to the counter and said to the girl taking the order: "Yeah, I'll have fries and a Chicken Special burger with no lettuce." The attendant gazed at him. "Would you like fries with that, sir?"

****

A bloke in a café late one evening called the waitress over and said, "You're really cute. I'd love to shag you." The waitress looked at him and said, "Look, I've been stood on my feet all day. I'm exhausted." The bloke shrugged, and said, "Great, let's go and lie down..."

****

This bloke picked up a tin of sweetcorn in a supermarket and looked at the label. "Contains no artificial additives or preservatives," it read. Then, a few inches below, was another message saying, "Contains reclaimed aluminium." The bloke showed the label to his wife and said, "Frankly, I'd rather have the additives..."

****

There was a restaurant that had a sign in the window which read, "Eat now - pay waiter."

****

A bloke went into a pizza parlour with a friend. Naturally they could not decide what type of pizza to get, so to save hours of pointless wrangling they decided to go half and half. "I'd like a large ham and mushroom pizza, please, but with extra pepperoni on one half." The dumb-looking guy behind the counter looked at him and asked, seriously, "Which half do you want the pepperoni put on?" Quick as a flash the bloke said, "Put it on the left-hand half." The guy at the desk duly wrote down, "Ham and mushroom, pepperoni on the left," and handed the order to the chef, who grinned and got on with making the pizza. About half an hour later, the guy at the desk called the bloke over to give him his pizza. When he got there, he noticed that the pepperoni half was facing him so, unable to resist, he said, "Hey, I wanted that pepperoni on the left, not on the bottom!" The desk guy looked upset, grabbed the pizza and with one swift motion threw it into the rubbish bin. "I'm really sorry, sir," he apologised. "I'll get the chef to make you another one..."

****

An elderly couple died in a car accident and found themselves being given a guided tour of heaven by Saint Peter himself. He took them to the area they would be living in, saying, "Over there is your beachside villa - the tennis courts and swimming pools are round the back; the community centre is down the road a bit, there's a pair of golf courses just past that hill, and if you feel hungry or thirsty, just drop by one of the pubs or restaurants. Everything is free, of course, and you'll find that you have plenty of energy if you do want to exercise. I know you'll be happy; everybody is." Then he smiled and flew off. The bloke turned to his wife and muttered, "Honestly, Alice. If you hadn't insisted on all that damn bran and low-fat milk, we could have been here 15 years ago!"

****

A Scotsman was in a restaurant. "How much do you charge for one single drop of whisky?" he asked the waitress. "That would be free, sir," she smiled. "Excellent," said the Scots bloke, "drip me a mugful."

Did you hear about the restaurant that had a sign in the window reading "Now Serving Food"? You really have to wonder what they used to serve...

There's a small snack-bar next to the atomic accelerator at CERN. It's called "The Fission Chips Café"!

A bloke was eating in a Polish restaurant when to his horror he found a dead cockroach at the bottom of his soup. He screamed for the waitress, "There's a cockroach in my soup!" She smiled, and said: "Eat. We have more. I bring you fork."

This guy was in a greasy spoon, drinking a cuppa, when he found a dead dormouse in the bottom of the cup, nestled among the tea-leaves. "Hey!" he yelled to the woman behind the counter, "What the hell is the meaning of this?" She looked at him and shouted back, "I ain't got no idea, love. I'm a London gal, not a gypsy!"

This Polish guy walked into a restaurant. "What would you like?" asked the waitress. "You know what I like," replied the man, "but first, we eat, yes?"

****

A bloke reading the menu in a small café called the waiter over. "Are you ready to order, sir?" asked the waiter. "I have a question," said the bloke. "Why do two hard-boiled eggs cost twice as much as a three-egg omelette?" "Ah," said the waiter, "Well, you can't count the eggs in an omelette..."

****

Being overweight is something that just sort of snacks up on you...

****

Dieting is the triumph of mind over platter. You just need to keep your willpower dominant over your won't power.

****

It was a brave man who ate the very first oyster...

****

There was a sign in the baker's window that read, "Cakes 66p. Upside-down cakes 99p"!

****

Scientists have discovered that we actually live on only about a third of what we eat. Health farms, gymnasiums and diet pill manufacturers live on the other two-thirds.

****

A new experimental car was designed that ran on used chip fat. It did 400 miles to the gallon and let off very few fumes, but you had to stop every twenty miles to change the vinegar.

****

There are many things on offer on restaurant menus around the world that perhaps aren't exactly what the kitchen staff had in mind. Even worse, some are...

Beef rashers beaten up in the country people's fashion	Poland
Buttered saucepans and fried hormones	Japan
Cock in wine	Cairo

Cold shredded children and sea blubber in spicy sauce	China
Dreaded veal cutlet with potatoes in cream	China
Fillet streak, popotoes, chocolate mouse	Hong Kong
French creeps	America
French fried ships	Cairo
Fried fishermen	Japan
Fried friendship	Nepal
Goose barnacles	Spain
Indonesian Nazi Goreng	Hong Kong
Lioness cutlet	Cairo
Lobster Thermos	Cairo
Muscles Of Marines	Cairo
Pork with fresh garbage	Vietnam
Prawn cock and tail	Cairo
Roasted duck let loose	Poland
Sole Bonne Femme (i.e. "Landlady Style")	France
Strawberry crap	Japan
Sweat from the trolley	Italy
Teppan Yaki, Before Your Cooked Right Eyes	Japan
Toes with butter and jam	Bali

Similarly, some products have a certain image problem:

Ass Glue	Chinese glue
Ban Cock	Indian cockroach repellent
Cat Wetty	Japanese moistened hand towels

Colon Plus	Spanish detergent
Creap Creamy Powder	Japanese coffee creamer
Crundy	Japanese gourmet candy
Homo Sausage	East Asian fish sausage
Hornyphon	Austrian video recorder
I'm Dripper	Japanese instant coffee
Last Climax	Japanese tissues
Libido	Chinese soda
My Fanny	Japanese toilet paper
Pipi	Yugoslavian orange drink
Pocari Sweat	Japanese sport drink
Polio	Czechoslovakian laundry detergent
Shitto	Ghanean pepper sauce
Superglans	Netherlands car wax
Swine	Chinese chocolates

The Day Today

Today

9

Topical Jokes Past and Present

What did OJ Simpson say to Ronald Goldman when he found the bloke with his ex-wife? "Hey, buddy; mind if I cut in?"

****

What do you call three days of filthy weather followed by bright sunshine? A bank holiday.

****

Chandran, a classical Indian dancer of some standing, has complained about an upcoming Spice Girls concert scheduled to be held near certain ancient Indian sculptures. Her protest is that the Spice Girls are "inappropriate for the locale." Rumour suggests she would think it far more suitable to have the Spice Girls dropped into a pit and then stoned to death.

****

Two men sentenced to die in the electric chair on the same day were led to the room in which they would meet their Maker. The priest had given them the last rites, a formal speech had been made by the warden and the final prayers had been said. The warden turned to the first bloke and with a grave expression on his face asked, "Well, son, do you have any last requests?" "Yes, sir, I do," replied the condemned man. "I love dance music. I really want to listen to the

Spice Girls for one last time before I die. Can that be organised?" "Of course," replied the warden. He then crossed to the second bloke, and asked, "How about you, son? Do you have a final request?" "God, yes," pleaded the prisoner, "Have mercy. Kill me first!"

****

As the new Welsh assembly gets ready to take over administrative affairs, a new white paper has been tabled suggesting that housing benefit could be extended to same-sex couples. Farmers are likely to be disappointed at the paper, which requires that the couples still have to be the same species.

****

Steven Spielberg was discussing his new project – an action document drama about famous composers starring top movie stars. Sylvester Stallone, Steven Segal, Bruce Willis, and Arnold Schwarzenegger were all present. Spielberg strongly desired the box office 'oomph' of these superstars, so he was prepared to let them choose whichever composer they would want to portray, as long as they were very famous. "Well," started Stallone, "I've always admired Mozart. I would love to play him." "Chopin has always been my favourite, and my image would improve if people saw me playing the piano" said Willis. "I'll play him." "I've always been partial to Strauss and his waltzes," said Segal. "I'd like to play him." Spielberg was very pleased with these choices. "Sounds splendid." Then, looking at Schwarzenegger, he asked, "Who do you want to be, Arnold?" So Arnold says, "I'll be Bach."

✳✳✳✳

John Wayne Bobbitt has turned to the church for solace, and been ordained as a minister in Las Vegas. Rumour has it, however, that his chapel has no organ...

✳✳✳✳

Reports from military intelligence sources say that Iraqi president Saddam Hussein has placed his wife under house arrest, and forbidden her to leave the palace. The presidential compound contains over 100 rooms, a bowling alley, indoor and outdoor pools and three satellite dishes. Civil liberties groups in the UK have condemned Hussein for subjecting his own wife to a regime even worse that than suffered by British convicts.

✳✳✳✳

Many commentators were astonished that Pan-Am could actually lose one of the engines from an aeroplane. It later transpired that the engine had a luggage sticker on it, and it was found, sad and lonely, on the baggage carousel at Karachi International.

****

A recent campaign calling for car safety awareness was launched with a national Child Car Safety Week. A spokesman said, "Over the course of this week we hope to make everyone think about the safety of children in cars. All children should wear a seatbelt. Then, next week, everyone can go back to slinging their kids through windscreens as normal."

****

Early reports suggest that at least six men have already died after using the new anti-impotence drug Viagra. Ironically, sales of the drug have been increased. One customer said that the fact it could keep men stiff indefinitely was a huge plus.

****

Rumour has it that Tony Blair and Paddy Ashdown are left-handed...That's peculiar for politicians because they are all, without exception, under-handed.

****

Notoriously stupid American politician Dan Quayle has announced that he will be standing for president, but he has yet to decide when.

One colleague close to Mr. Quayle has said campaign officials are praying that it happens to be a year when there's an election on.

✳✳✳✳

The stock market may be bad, but I slept like a baby all through the Black Friday crash and its aftermath. Every hour, on the hour, I woke up crying.

✳✳✳✳

How does Michael Jackson pick his nose? By catalogue...

✳✳✳✳

Florida was recently submerged under a huge blanket of smog, causing officials to issue the first ever state-wide health alert. Residents have been advised against all strenuous outdoors activity, including gardening, jogging, beach-ball and slaughtering British tourists.

✳✳✳✳

What do you get when you cross a lesbian with a draft dodger? Chelsea Clinton.

George Tenet, Director of the CIA, has been called before the American Congress to explain why US intelligence forces were unaware that India and Pakistan were both about to start detonating nuclear weapons. Reports suggest that Tenet blamed the lapse on the workload involved in finding and killing all of Bill Clinton's former business associates, adding, "We've got most of them now, though, so soon it'll be business as usual."

****

The Hindenburg was in fact very similar to Waco in Texas. When push came to shove, both proved to contain flammable compounds.

****

David Koresh had a lot of wives, it's true, but they were all excellent matches.

****

The former president of the Swiss National Bank, Markus Lusser, died recently at the age of 67. His family have announced their plans to bury him in a secret grave somewhere in Zurich, marked only by a long string of coded numbers.

In the wake of the Challenger shuttle disaster, NASA are said to have banned a particular brand of canned drink from their bases - 7 Up.

****

The Colombian navy recently discovered a ship transporting more than a ton of cocaine out of the country in direct violation of Colombian law. Under current directives, no vessel is allowed to leave Colombia carrying less than three tons of coke.

****

What's the difference between OJ Simpson and Christopher Reeve? OJ hit the ground running and then walked away, while Christopher Reeve got the electric chair.

****

Singer George Michael was recently arrested and charged with performing a lewd act in a Beverley Hills public toilet. Music critics have hailed the event as a breakthrough for George Michael, saying that it's the first time ever that he has been more humiliated than former Wham partner Andrew Ridgely. Meanwhile, in the States, the pop star has been busily turning the event into a PR coup for himself. Like Hugh Grant before him, it appears that the Americans will forgive any pervert, so long as they've got a British accent.

****

Right-wing politicians have recently defended tobacco advertising, saying that kids don't start smoking because of posters, but because of stars like Leonardo DiCaprio smoking in high-impact films such as Titanic. There is of course no proof of this, but since the release of the film there has been a marked increase in the numbers of gay American teenagers shagging fat English girls as part of an attempt to prove that they're heterosexual.

****

In a vital boost for the Internet recently, several countries have agreed not to tax it, in order to help increase the prominence of electronic commerce and to foster the growth of a truly world-wide communications network. Consumer groups have hailed the move as a great breakthrough, saying, "An Internet tax could have been disastrous. Most 11-year-olds are already strapped for cash, and would have real difficulty coping with any further rises in their weekly hardcore pornography bills."

****

Elton John was recently knighted by the Queen. Interviewed after the event, Sir Elton said that it felt odd to get down on his knees only to end up not swallowing the sword.

****

A worrying new study has linked women's alcohol consumption with breast cancer, suggesting that women who get drunk regularly are more likely to suffer from the disease. The effects of this may be counterbalanced, however, by the fact that drunk women are likely to get their tits felt by a wide variety of blokes, and some of them could be doctors.

****

Bob Hope, the 95-year-old legend of comedy, has been knighted by the Queen. Hope, who was born in Britain, has been suffering from ill-health for some time. When told to kneel before the Queen, Hope was heard to mutter in confusion: "Bing? Is that you? I heard you were dead."

****

In 1969 the Apollo 11 mission went to the moon and sent back live images of Neil Armstrong and Buzz Aldrin bouncing around on the surface. More recently, in 1997, a special probe to Mars passed back images of the red planet's surface live as scientists sent the little buggy around the place. Why the fuck then can Channel Five not get a signal from the transmitter down the road to my house?

****

Sources indicate that Madonna, the bad girl of rock and roll, has started studying the Qaballah, an ancient form of Jewish mystical occultism. One commentator expressed no surprise, saying, "After you hit 40, have a kid and lose your interest in sex, becoming Jewish is the next logical step."

****

An evil-tempered old farmer died and went down to Hell. A couple of weeks later the Devil checked up on him and noticed that he didn't seem to be suffering like the rest of the damned souls. He checked the gauges and observed that the room was set to 80% humidity and a temperature of 28 degrees, so went in and said to the farmer, "What are you so cheerful about?" The farmer grinned and said, "I like it here. It's just like ploughing my fields in June." Well, that pissed the Devil off, so he went back to the controls and turned it to 90% humidity and a temperature of 32 degrees. He then went back to check the farmer again, who was standing around happy as a sandboy. "Oh, honestly," thought the Devil. "What are you so damn cheerful about now, then?" he asked the farmer. "This is even better," replied the farmer. "It's like tugging weeds out of the fields in July, except that my back's not breaking." Well, the Devil was even more pissed off, so he went to the controls and reset them yet again - 99% humidity and 40 degrees. When he looked in, the farmer was still grinning broadly. With a sinking feeling, the Devil asked him what this reminded him of. "Oh, it's just like spending the day in the grain silo in the middle of August," replied the farmer. Suddenly the Devil had a brainwave, thought, "I'm going to sort out this smug little wanker," and went to the controls, where he turned the temperature to minus ten degrees. Well, sure enough, at that humidity it started snowing. "We'll see what happy summers this reminds the fucker of now!" thought the Devil. He went back, only to find the farmer leaping up and down and shouting for joy. "Yes! Away the Gunners! Arsenal have finally won the Premiership!"

****

Pol Pot, the evil Cambodian dictator, is finally dead. The leader of the Khmer Rouge, his reign saw the murder of more than a million intellectuals and urbanites in an attempt to turn Cambodia into a nation of farmers. He eventually realised his mistake and repented after being forced to listen to 12 hours of The Archers non-stop.

****

Mikhail Gorbachev, the former leader of the USSR responsible for the dismantling of the communist system, has reportedly received $1 million as payment for acting in a Pizza Hut advert. Pizza Hut officials commented that Mr Gorbachev was the perfect choice, as he already had a splodge of tomato sauce on his forehead.

****

Recent discoveries of ancient primate remains suggest that humans evolved in several different places at the same time. That fits predictive models based on the British political system - a close look at Whitehall, the Houses of Parliament, Downing Street and Buckingham Palace clearly shows that there is all sorts of monkey business going on all over the place.

****

Elizabeth Taylor, the legendary 66-year-old actress, was recently hospitalised following a fall in which she injured her hip. Doctors said that Miss Taylor was extremely fortunate, and that her injuries would have been much worse if her fall had not been cushioned by her revoltingly saggy tits.

****

Word has it that Michael Jackson, the world's first trans-racial, is about to release a new book. The working title (allegedly) is, "The Ins and Outs of Child Rearing."

****

In these up-and-down market periods there is one sure-fire way to secure the attention of your broker. Snap your fingers in the air and call, "Waiter! Waiter!"

This bloke was in Devon, walking along a country path, when he noticed a young lad over to one side busy making something. He took a closer look, and was horrified to see that the boy was playing with cow manure. A bit taken aback, he went over and said, "What on earth are you doing, lad?" The boy looked up and said, "I'm making John Prescott." Amazed, and unable to think of anything sensible to say, he asked "Prescott? Why are you making John Prescott? Why not Tony Blair?" The boy looked at him seriously and said, "Oh no, I could never make Tony Blair." "Really? Why's that?" asked the man. The lad shrugged, and replied, "Come off it. There's not enough bullshit in all of Devon to make Tony Blair."

****

What's the difference between a pigeon and a stockbroker the day after Black Friday? Well, the pigeon can still put a deposit on a new Merc.

****

Unemployed French citizens occupied government buildings recently as part of a protest movement demanding greater social security benefits. The disturbance was quickly settled however, when the French government appealed to the Germans to send the tanks back in.

Lorena Bobbitt visited Equador, where the President treated her like his very own long-lost sister. To be fair though, can you imagine any bloke not wanting to be careful around her?

****